DISCIPLES PATH®

THE JOURNEY

VOLUME 4

LifeWay Press®
Nashville, Tennessee

DISCIPLES PATH

Disciples Path is a series of studies founded on Jesus' model of discipleship. Created by experienced disciple makers across the nation, it offers an intentional pathway for transformational discipleship and a way to help followers of Christ move from new disciples to mature disciple makers. Each study in the series is built on the principles of modeling, practicing, and multiplying:

- Leaders model the life of a biblical disciple.
- Disciples follow and practice from the leader.
- Disciples become disciple makers and multiply through the *Disciples Path*.

Each study in the series has been written and approved by disciple makers for small groups and one-on-one settings.

For helps on how to use *Disciples Path,* tips on how to better lead groups, or additional ideas for leading this study, visit: *ministrygrid.com/web/disciplespath*

Item: 005790764 • ISBN: 978-1-4300-6329-2

Eric Geiger
Vice President, LifeWay Resources

Sam O'Neal, Joel Polk
Content Editors

Michael Kelley
Director, Groups Publishing

We believe that the Bible has God for its author; salvation for its end; and truth, without any mixture of error, for its matter and that all Scripture is totally true and trustworthy. To review LifeWay's doctrinal guideline, visit *lifeway.com/doctrinalguideline.*

To order additional copies of this resource, write to LifeWay Resources Customer Service; One LifeWay Plaza; Nashville, TN 37234-0113; fax 615.251.5933; call toll free 800.458.2772; order online at *lifeway.com;* email *orderentry@lifeway.com;* or visit the LifeWay Christian Store serving you.

Printed in the United States of America

Groups Ministry Publishing; LifeWay Resources
One LifeWay Plaza; Nashville, TN 37234-0152

CONTENTS

HOW TO USE THIS RESOURCE

Welcome to *Disciples Path: The Journey*. In Volume 4 you'll continue to explore biblical stories of disciple-making and replication in order to gain a better understanding of what it means to follow Christ. As you get started, consider the following guides and suggestions for making the most of this experience.

GROUP DISCUSSION

Because the process of discipleship always involves at least two people—the leader and the disciple—each session of *Disciples Path: The Journey* includes a practical plan for group engagement and discussion.

This plan includes the following steps:

- **GET STARTED.** The first section of the group material helps you ease into the discussion by starting on common ground. You'll begin by reflecting on the previous session and your recent experiences as a disciple. After spending time in prayer, you'll find a practical illustration to help you launch into the main topic of the current session.

- **THE STORY.** While using *Disciples Path: The Journey*, you'll find opportunities to engage the Bible through both story and teaching. That's why the group time for each session features two main sections: **Know the Story** and **Unpack the Story. Know the Story** introduces a biblical text and includes follow-up questions for brief discussion. It's recommended that your group encounter the biblical text by reading it out loud. **Unpack the Story** includes practical teaching material and discussion questions—both designed to help you engage the truths contained in the biblical text. To make the most of your experience, use the provided material as a launching point for deeper conversation. As you read through the teaching material and engage the questions as a group, be thinking of how the truths you're exploring will impact your everyday life.

- **ENGAGE.** The group portion of each session ends with an activity designed to help you practice the biblical principles introduced in **Know the Story** and more fully explored in **Unpack the Story.** This part of the group time often appeals to different learning styles and will push you to engage the text at a personal level.

INDIVIDUAL DISCOVERY

Each session of *Disciples Path: The Journey* also includes content for individual use during the time between group gatherings. This content is divided into three categories:

Worship: features content for worship and devotion. These activities provide opportunities for you to connect with God in meaningful ways and deepen your relationship with Him.

Personal study: features content for personal study. These pages help you gain a deeper understanding of the truths and principles explored during the group discussion.

Application: features content for practical application. These suggestions help you take action based on the information you've learned and your encounters with God.

Note: Aside from the **Reading Plan,** the content provided in the Individual Discovery portion of each session should be considered optional. You'll get the most out of your personal study by working with your group leader to create a personalized discipleship plan using the **Weekly Activities** checklist included in each session.

ADDITIONAL SUGGESTIONS

- You'll be best prepared for each group discussion or mentoring conversation if you read the session material beforehand. A serious read will serve you most effectively, but skimming the **Get Started** and **The Story** sections will also be helpful if time is limited.

- The deeper you're willing to engage in the group discussions and individual discovery each session, the more you'll benefit from those experiences. Don't hold back, and don't be afraid to ask questions whenever necessary.

- As you explore the **Engage** portion of each session, you'll have the chance to practice different activities and spiritual disciplines. Take advantage of the chance to observe others during the group time—and to ask questions—so that you'll be prepared to incorporate these activities into your private spiritual life as well.

SESSION 1

RETURN TO THE GOSPEL

Because the gospel is the driving force behind the Christian life, we must consistently return to its message.

GET STARTED

REFLECT

Welcome to Volume 4 of *Disciples Path: The Journey!* This entire resource is meant to be more like a circle than a straight line. While it's true that we're all moving forward in maturity as disciples of Jesus, we must constantly come back to the core of what drives us onward: the gospel.

We must do so not only for our own sake, but for the sake of others. That's because the pathway of discipleship is one in which we're always meant to be bringing others along with us. So, when we return to the beginning again and again, we not only remember the core of what discipleship is, we're also reminded of the importance of obeying Jesus' command.

To be a disciple is to make disciples. The beginning and the fuel of both of those things is the gospel.

Think back over the course of your own discipleship journey. Why is it important to come back to the gospel again and again?

What might happen to us spiritually if we fail to do so?

How does doing so help us embrace Jesus' command to make disciples?

PRAY

Begin this session by connecting with God through prayer. Use the following guidelines as you speak with Him together:

- Thank God again today for the simple message of the gospel, by which we are saved from our sins.
- Ask the Lord to keep you from prideful thoughts that might lead you to believe you've moved past your need for the gospel.
- Pray that as you engage the Scripture, the Lord would give you a fresh response to the gospel.

INTRODUCTION

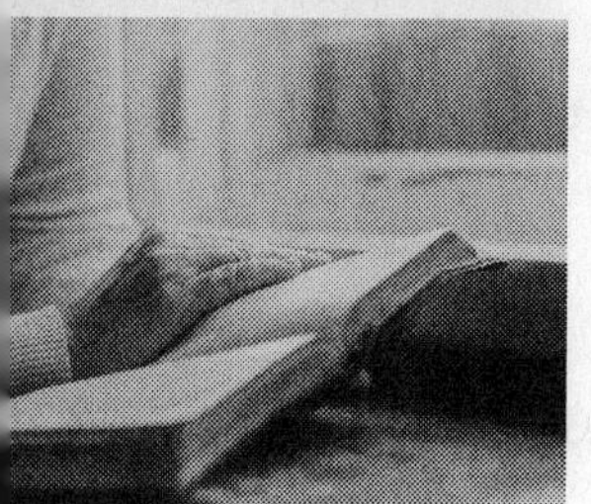

If you've ever run track or even watched an Olympic race, you know the importance of the starting blocks. Most races, especially sprints, are decided by the tiniest of margins—literally fractions of seconds. The winner is often determined not at the end of the race, but at the beginning; it's all about who can get out of the blocks the fastest.

The starting blocks, then, must be firmly placed. They must be stable and steady and provide a good foothold for the runner to push off. If the blocks are indeed stable and steady, the runner will be able to achieve that great start which often leads to victory.

Many disciples think of the gospel—the message that Jesus Christ lived a perfect life and died to bear the weight of sin's punishment in our place—like the starting blocks of the Christian life. This message is what we initially believe, and like the starting blocks, we brace ourselves against it to then run the race of discipleship.

But it's a mistake to think of the gospel in this way. True enough, the gospel is the entrance point for the life of discipleship, but it's more than that. The gospel isn't just the beginning, but it's the fuel by which we run and the certainty of the prize at the end. In other words, the gospel is not only the starting blocks, but the track itself.

Can you remember the first time you heard the message of the gospel? How did you initially respond?

Have you viewed the gospel more as the starting blocks or the track for your spiritual life? Explain.

In this session, we will seek to once again encounter the message of the gospel. In so doing, we'll also discover why the gospel must be returned to again and again, because it is the driving force behind our entire lives as disciples of Jesus.

KNOW THE STORY

Paul the apostle had a very clear pattern in his ministry. His goal was to go to places where no one had ever heard of Jesus, share with those people the message of forgiveness and restoration through Christ, begin a fellowship of believers in that city, establish local disciple-making leadership, and then move on to start over again.

Much of the New Testament consists of letters that the apostle Paul wrote back to churches he was in relationship with, many which he himself had a hand in starting. This is the case for the letters to the Corinthians.

Unfortunately, the Corinthian churches had drifted into all kinds of disobedience in Paul's absence, and so he had to write them not only about specific issues in their church, but also to bring them back to the core of their faith.

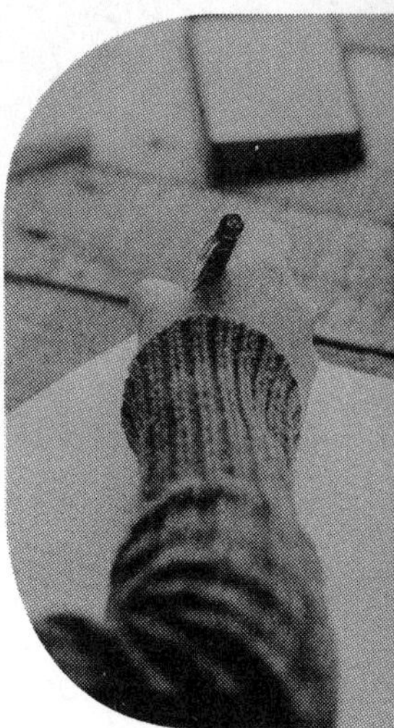

> 1 Now I want to make clear for you, brothers and sisters, the
> gospel I preached to you, which you received, on which you have
> taken your stand 2 and by which you are being saved, if you hold
> to the message I preached to you—unless you believed in vain.
> 3 For I passed on to you as most important what I also received:
> that Christ died for our sins according to the Scriptures, 4 that
> he was buried, that he was raised on the third day according
> to the Scriptures, 5 and that he appeared to Cephas, then to
> the Twelve. 6 Then he appeared to over five hundred brothers
> and sisters at one time; most of them are still alive, but some
> have fallen asleep. 7 Then he appeared to James, then to all the
> apostles. 8 Last of all, as to one born at the wrong time, he also
> appeared to me.
> 1 CORINTHIANS 15:1-8

What do these verses teach about the gospel?

What is it about the gospel message that makes it "most important"?

UNPACK THE STORY

FAMILY AND CLARITY

As Paul began this section of his letter, there are two key terms for us to notice. The first is "brothers and sisters"—a term that none of the New Testament writers would have used lightly. The term doesn't necessarily indicate a blood relationship, but a spiritual one. Because of the gospel, Christians have been brought into one family that extends beyond our earthly family. It also extends beyond race, culture, nationality, or any other form of human dividing line. We are brothers and sisters in faith.

By using this term, Paul reminded us that the Corinthians, his original audience, were already part of the family of faith. We, too, must be reminded again and again that we are a part of this same family.

How would this message benefit the Corinthians if they were already disciples of Jesus?

Because of the gospel, Christians have been brought into one family that extends beyond our earthly family.

The second term for us to notice is "make clear." Did Paul want obedience from the Corinthians? Certainly. Did he want them to resolve the differences in their church? Absolutely. But he knew that any obedience or unity or anything else that wasn't informed and fueled by a clear understanding of the gospel would ultimately be short-lived.

Like the Corinthians, we as modern-day disciples have many competing interests. We are real people with real jobs, real families, and real responsibilities. In the midst of all the other details of life, the gospel can easily be put in the backseat, or even muddled together with something else. For example, we might begin to think that believing in Jesus will result in God giving us all kinds of material benefits—money, power, prestige, good health, and so on. Or, we might begin to think that we contribute to our own salvation in Christ by performing good deeds.

When have you seen the message of the gospel become muddled or confused with other worldviews?

In any of these cases, Paul has a good word for us. It's a word for us as brothers and sisters, and it's a word of clarity.

RECEIVED AND STANDING

Paul went on to remind the Corinthians, and now us, that this message of the gospel is what saves us. People are always susceptible to pride, but the true and clear gospel leaves no doubt about who gets the credit for our salvation: it's by faith alone in Christ alone. Still, our egos are easily inflatable, and if we're not careful, we might begin to subtly demand some of the glory that is rightfully meant for God alone.

We are the recipients of the gospel and salvation through Christ, and remembering that truth puts us in a humble posture before the Lord. When we're in that humble posture, we're in the right position to continue to receive our spiritual nourishment from Him, trusting in Him for all things. And because we're trusting in Him for all things, it makes sense that the gospel is not only what we received, but also that which we are now standing on.

In other words, when it's rightly understood, the gospel becomes the basis for every decision, emotion, and action in our lives.

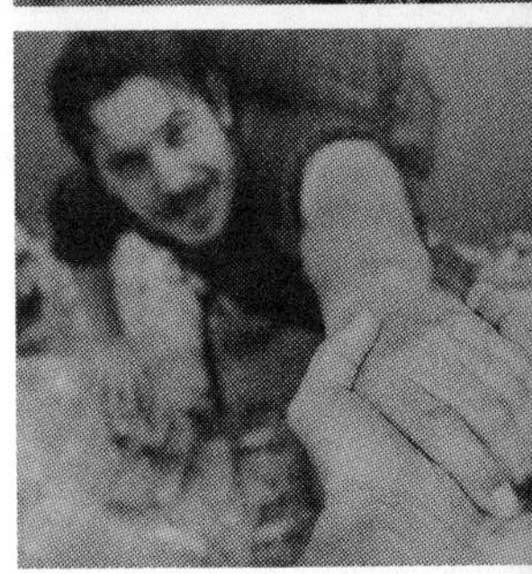

How do we make sure we're standing on the gospel?

How has the gospel influenced your life in recent weeks?

What are practical ways we can remind ourselves of the gospel message each day?

When it's rightly understood, the gospel becomes the basis for every decision, emotion, and action in our lives.

What, then, is the gospel? Paul laid it out succinctly and clearly for us:

- The gospel is the message of the death and resurrection of Jesus. Without His death, there is no forgiveness of sin. And without the resurrection, there can be no eternal life for any of us.
- The gospel is "according to the Scriptures." This wasn't a spur-of-the-moment decision on the part of God, but rather His plan all along for our salvation and redemption.
- The gospel is verifiable. We don't have a blind faith. Paul knew that literally hundreds of witnesses could testify about the resurrected Christ. We can trust in a historically verified message when we trust in the gospel.

ENGAGE

We must remind ourselves and others daily of the clear gospel by which we were saved and on which we are now standing. Because no one drifts towards Jesus and the gospel, only away from Jesus and the gospel, we must be vigilant to remember these things of first importance.

List three practical ways you will remind yourself daily of the gospel.

1.

2.

3.

When was the last time you had a conversation with someone that revolved around the gospel? Consider that you have the opportunity to do what Paul did for the Corinthians: remind someone else of that which is of first importance.

PRAYER REQUESTS

WEEKLY ACTIVITIES

In addition to studying God's Word, work with your group leader to create a plan for personal study, worship, and application between now and the next session. Select from the following optional activities to match your personal preferences and available time.

Worship

- [x] Read your Bible. Complete the reading plan on page 14.
- [ ] Spend time with God by engaging the devotional experience on page 15.

Personal Study

- [ ] Read and interact with "No Plan B" on page 16.
- [ ] Read and interact with "No Blind Faith" on page 18.

Application

- [ ] Memorize 1 Corinthians 15:3-5: "For I passed on to you as most important what I also received: that Christ died for our sins according to the Scriptures, that he was buried, that he was raised on the third day according to the Scriptures, and that he appeared to Cephas, then to the Twelve."
- [ ] Imagine you only have five minutes to share with someone that which is most important. Create a script for yourself based on Paul's description of the gospel in 1 Corinthians 15.
- [ ] With the help of your spouse or a good friend, do a "life evaluation" this week. Consider whether you're truly standing on the gospel in the major parts of your life.
- [ ] Continue journaling during your prayer times, writing down what God tells you concerning your walk with Him.
- [ ] Other:

READING PLAN

Read through the following Scripture passages this week. Use the space provided to record your thoughts and responses.

Day 1
Acts 2:22-36

Day 2
Romans 10:14-17

Day 3
Isaiah 53:1-12

Day 4
Psalm 22:1-31

Day 5
Philippians 2:1-11

Day 6
1 Corinthians 15:50-58

Day 7
1 Peter 1:3-12

BEGIN AGAIN—AGAIN

We are by nature a dissatisfied people. We tend to constantly worry that we're missing out on something with someone somewhere. Such an attitude becomes a big problem when it affects our spiritual life.

Disciples of Jesus never move past the gospel; we only move deeper into it. God isn't holding out on us, waiting to reveal some secret knowledge when we've proven ourselves worthy. If we have believed the gospel, then we have the very best God has to offer.

The pathway of discipleship is rooted and grounded in the confident faith that God has proven His love for us through the death and resurrection of Jesus. When we accept that message by faith, we are included in the family of God and are granted all the spiritual blessings God has to offer us in Christ. Part of the discipline of spiritual growth is coming back to this core truth over and over again.

When we feel like God is holding out on us, we come back to the gospel. When we wonder if there is something we're missing, we come back to the gospel. When we doubt whether God will continue His work in and through us, we come back to the gospel.

The disciple of Jesus knows what it means to begin again—again.

When have you felt like God was holding out on you?

How can remembering the gospel make us more confident in God's love and generosity toward us?

Do you find it easy or difficult to believe the gospel right now? Why?

What are you afraid of or anxious about at this point in life? How can remembering the gospel be a remedy for your worry and fear?

NO PLAN B

Some people look at the Bible as two distinct parts. In the first part, the Old Testament, they see a God who is all about wrath and judgment. In the second part, the New Testament, they see a God who is more about grace and love. It's important as we grow as disciples that we don't carry or contribute to this misunderstanding.

How did you process the differences in the Old and New Testaments when you first started studying the Bible?

How do you understand those differences now?

God is who He is. And He is who He will always be.

One of the ways we know this to be true is because the gospel of Jesus Christ was not God's Plan B. If we drift into thinking of the "mean God" of the Old Testament and the "nice God" of the New Testament, we might also be tempted to think that the reason Jesus had to die was because God's first plan didn't work.

What are some possible dangers of believing that Jesus' death and resurrection wasn't always part of God's plan?

It wasn't that God was wringing His hands in heaven, trying to decide what to do about all these humans who were destined for an eternity in hell because of their sin, and then He had a stroke of genius and came up with the idea of the crucifixion and resurrection. It certainly wasn't that God temporarily lost control of this world, and while He was out of control, men seized their moment and tragically executed His Son. Instead, what we know from the Old Testament is that the cross and resurrection of Jesus has always been God's plan—His only plan.

Consider just one passage from the prophets that demonstrates this reality:

[2] He grew up before him like a young plant
and like a root out of dry ground.
He didn't have an impressive form
or majesty that we should look at him,
no appearance that we should desire him.
[3] He was despised and rejected by men,
a man of suffering who knew what sickness was.
He was like someone people turned away from;
he was despised, and we didn't value him.
[4] Yet he himself bore our sicknesses,
and he carried our pains;
but we in turn regarded him stricken,
struck down by God, and afflicted.
[5] But he was pierced because of our rebellion,
crushed because of our iniquities;
punishment for our peace was on him,
and we are healed by his wounds.
ISAIAH 53:2-5

This passage, written hundreds of years before Christ was born, shows the intent of God. Because the gospel was planned beforehand, we can be confident that God doesn't change His mind. And we can know that nothing—not a single thing—is out of His control.

The gospel is Plan A. It always has been.

How does knowing that the gospel is not a backup plan give us confidence in God's wisdom and love?

Is there a particular situation in your life right now in which you need to trust in the wisdom of God? Write a prayer below that articulates that trust.

PERSONAL STUDY 2

NO BLIND FAITH

It has been said before that Christianity is a crutch for the weak. That phrase is intended to be an insult, charging that Christians believe in the ridiculous and illogical, and that they do so because they aren't strong enough to accept the logical and rational. It's supposed to imply that Christians aren't strong enough to deal with reality; therefore, we to resort to myths and fairy tales.

Among other things, 1 Corinthians 15 reminds us that we don't subscribe to that kind of blind and ridiculous faith. Rather, this passage helps us know that the resurrection of Jesus Christ is one of the most validated occurrences in history.

In a modern court of law, the clincher for confirming a suspect's guilt or innocence is the testimony of an eyewitness. Beyond that, all evidence is suspect; it's merely circumstantial. But if the prosecution or defense can produce someone who, with their own eyes, can testify about the truth of a situation, then the case is either made or broken.

We even have a cultural saying about it—when an eyewitnesses confirms something beyond a shadow of a doubt, we say it's "gospel" or "the gospel truth."

Look again at what Paul wrote in 1 Corinthians 15:

> [5] and that he appeared to Cephas, then to the Twelve. [6] Then he appeared
> to over five hundred brothers and sisters at one time; most of them are
> still alive, but some have fallen asleep. [7] Then he appeared to James, then
> to all the apostles. [8] Last of all, as to one born at the wrong time, he also
> appeared to me.
>
> 1 CORINTHIANS 15:5-8

How do these verses present evidence for Jesus' resurrection?

How strong is this evidence in your mind? Explain.

How would you present or explain that evidence to others?

It's interesting that Paul specifically mentioned Jesus appeared to "five hundred brothers and sisters," and that most of them were "still alive" at the time of Paul's letter. Paul wanted to point out that many of these witnesses were still alive for the simple reason that any of the Corinthians, or anyone else for that matter, could talk to them about it.

In other words, they didn't have to rely on blind faith.

As a disciple of Jesus, you can go forth today in confidence not only because you know that God has changed your heart through the gospel, but that the death and resurrection of Jesus is validated by witnesses. This is no blind faith. Our hope is much more certain than that.

When are some times that you have doubted whether the gospel is true or not? What helped you get through those times of doubt?

Can doubt actually be a good thing for disciples of Jesus? Why or why not?

If you were discipling someone who struggled with doubt, what advice would you give that person?

Is Christianity a crutch for the weak? In many ways, the answer is yes—not because our faith lacks evidence, but because all of us are weak in and of ourselves. None of us has the strength or ability to save ourselves from the consequences of our sin.

The gospel is much more than our "crutch'; it's an incredible gift that offers our only hope for salvation. It's the driving force behind everything we are and everything we do as disciples of Jesus. Therefore, let us return to the gospel again and again as we follow Him.

SESSION 2

SEE THE BIG PICTURE

Every portion of the Bible contains the plan and work of redemption.

GET STARTED

REFLECT

Last session, we went back to the beginning of every disciple's path—to the gospel. We saw that far from being the opening to the Christian life, the gospel is also the fuel and motivation for how we continue to grow in Christ. We never move past the gospel. Just as Paul reminded the Corinthian Christians about that which is of most importance, so must we remind ourselves of the gospel every day.

In this session, we'll discover how the message of the gospel is actually the central message of all Scripture. As we engage the big picture of God's Word, we'll see that even the Old Testament casts the shadow of the cross.

Before we move forward, reflect back on what you learned and put into practice in recent days:

Which of the assignments did you explore this week? How did it go?

What did you learn or experience while reading the Bible?

What questions would you like to ask?

PRAY

Begin this session by connecting with God through prayer. Use the following guidelines as you speak with Him together:

- Thank God that the gospel is for you both today and every day.
- Pray that the Lord would continue to open your eyes to how central the gospel is not only to all of Scripture, but also to every component of everyday life.
- Pray that as you engage the Scriptures today, you will, like the travelers you study, have a fresh experience and vision of Jesus.

INTRODUCTION

In the mid-1990's one of the fads that swept popular culture was the introduction of 3D posters of various sizes. At first glance, each of these prints looked like a series of repeated lines, dots, and shapes. But if you relaxed your eyes and continued to stare at the pictures in a certain way, the individual images would fade away to reveal a larger image popping up from within.

It wasn't magic; just clever printing. The creators were able to obscure an image that had been there all the time beneath the pattern of the print. While each individual shape was its own picture, they all came together to form something much greater.

It's the same concept, in essence, that's used in an artistic style called mosaic. This is a creative medium where the artist uses individual tiles to eventually be placed in just the right pattern to create one larger image.

In both cases, the point is the same: a person can study the smaller, individual tiles or shapes, but if they do, they lose the whole point of the larger picture. The whole point is the picture behind the picture—one that can only be seen when the entire image is in view.

In a similar way, there's a picture behind the pictures within the Bible. While the Bible is full of individual stories of kingdoms, wars, plagues, deliverance, heroes, and prophets, there is a larger picture that all these individual pieces come together to form. The larger picture is that of God's ongoing plan of redemption, centered on the death and the resurrection of Jesus Christ.

How would you summarize the central message of the Bible in a single sentence?

Why is it important for disciples of Jesus to understand the central message of Scripture?

In this session, we'll find the resurrected Christ opening up the eyes of two travelers so they can understand the holistic message of the Bible. We'll also pray that God will do the same for us.

KNOW THE STORY

Jesus had been crucified. He'd been buried in a tomb, and His remaining disciples were in disarray. As we examine Luke 24, we find two of those disciples traveling together on the road to Emmaus on what we now understand to be the first Easter Sunday. The travelers were joined by Jesus Himself, although they did not recognize Him at first.

As they journeyed together, Jesus showed them that He was—and is and always will be—the central character of the Bible.

> 25 He said to them, "How foolish and slow you are to believe all
> that the prophets have spoken! 26 Wasn't it necessary for the
> Messiah to suffer these things and enter into his glory?" 27 Then
> beginning with Moses and all the Prophets, he interpreted for
> them the things concerning himself in all the Scriptures.
>
> 28 They came near the village where they were going, and he
> gave the impression that he was going farther. 29 But they urged
> him, "Stay with us, because it's almost evening, and now the
> day is almost over." So he went in to stay with them.
>
> 30 It was as he reclined at the table with them that he took the
> bread, blessed and broke it, and gave it to them. 31 Then their
> eyes were opened, and they recognized him, but he disappeared
> from their sight. 32 They said to each other, "Weren't our hearts
> burning within us while he was talking with us on the road and
> explaining the Scriptures to us?" 33 That very hour they got up
> and returned to Jerusalem. They found the Eleven and those
> with them gathered together, 34 who said, "The Lord has truly
> been raised and has appeared to Simon!" 35 Then they began to
> describe what had happened on the road and how he was made
> known to them in the breaking of the bread.
>
> LUKE 24:25-35

When have you experienced the miracle of God's Word in a new and powerful way?

UNPACK THE STORY

THE ONGOING JOURNEY

The two disciples in this story were on a journey of revelation. The further they traveled together, the more they learned about Jesus and His central place in God's Word.

As they began their journey, they weren't even convinced of Jesus' true identity. In light of the crucifixion, they viewed Jesus as a powerful prophet, but nothing more (see Luke 24:19). Further, they had not yet realized that the death of Jesus was part of God's plan for redemption. They viewed the crucifixion as a terrible tragedy perpetrated by evil and jealous leaders (see 24:20).

At points in our spiritual journeys, we also may have doubts about who Jesus is in the universe. We might become confused about His identity, His power, or His mission. But as we continue to walk forward, God will continue to open our eyes to the truth of Jesus' identity—just as He did for these disciples.

In order to grow in our relationship with Jesus, we must not look to popular opinion or other human means for clarity about Him.

What are some of the ways your understanding of Jesus has changed and grown over time?

God isn't hiding from His people. If you're a Christ-follower, then the Holy Spirit lives inside you. One of the reasons He's there is to help you grow in knowledge, intimacy, and obedience toward Jesus.

However, this text also shows us that in order to grow in our relationship with Jesus, we must not look to popular opinion or other human means for clarity about Him. Instead, we must return to Scripture again and again.

That's where we find the revelation of God once and for all.

What gives you confidence in the value of God's Word?

What gives you confidence that all of God's Word is valuable?

THE CENTRAL MESSAGE

It's important to remember that there was no New Testament at the time these disciples walked with Jesus; those books had not yet been written. But the Old Testament was more than adequate for Jesus to explain God's plan for redemption—His whole plan.

The text tells us that Jesus started all the way back with Moses, the giver of the law, and then worked His way through the prophets. We can imagine Jesus explaining that the law was impossible to keep, but was meant to reveal the character of God and point everyone to their great need of grace. We can hear Him in our minds walking through the prophetic passages of the Old Testament, showing time and time again how God was completely in control—all the way to that moment when Jesus was nailed to the cross. No doubt the men's mouths were hanging open as they continued to walk, for verse upon verse had suddenly come alive to them in a brand new way.

When we read the Bible today, we must read individual portions of Scripture in light of the whole. All of Scripture reveals God's plan of redemption through Jesus Christ. For that reason, when we seek to understand and apply what we find in God's Word, we must constantly be coming back to this central theme. We should be asking, "What does this passage show me about God's plan of redemption through Jesus Christ?"

When we discipline ourselves to read, study, and meditate on Scripture in this way, our whole focus begins to change. We no longer see ourselves as the center of the universe, and we no longer see the Bible as being about us and our lives. Instead, we approach Scripture with a Jesus-centered perspective. We then come to understand that discipleship isn't finding out how Jesus fits into the story of our lives, but rather submitting our desires so that we might find our place in His life.

All of Scripture reveals God's plan of redemption through Jesus Christ.

How would you describe your typical motivations for reading and studying God's Word?

What are some practical ways to incorporate the full picture of the Scriptures into your discipline of personal study? Into a group study?

ENGAGE

In a way, all of us are on the road to Emmaus. Day by day as we walk with Jesus, He will be faithful to show us more and more truth about who He is and what He is doing. But that truth will come not from mere opinion or hearsay; it will come only from God's Word.

We don't have to conduct our study alone, however. When we engage in exploring God's Word with God's people, we continue to grow in our knowledge of Him. Sometimes we even multiply our understanding (and our growth) by joining together.

In light of these truths, work together as a group to make a plan for how you will study the Scriptures together in the months to come. Specifically, how will you structure your study and discussion times once you have completed *Disciples Path: The Journey?*

PRAYER REQUESTS

WEEKLY ACTIVITIES

In addition to studying God's Word, work with your group leader to create a plan for personal study, worship, and application between now and the next session. Select from the following optional activities to match your personal preferences and available time.

Worship

- [x] Read your Bible. Complete the reading plan on page 28.
- [ ] Spend time with God by engaging the devotional experience on page 29.

Personal Study

- [ ] Read and interact with "Shadows of What's to Come" on page 30.
- [ ] Read and interact with "Just One Hero" on page 32.

Application

- [ ] Memorize Luke 24:27: "Then beginning with Moses and all the Prophets, he interpreted for them the things concerning himself in all the Scriptures."
- [ ] The disciples on the road were in a position to hear from Jesus. What are some practical ways you can make room in your life to listen more closely to Jesus' voice? Do so for at least ten minutes each day.
- [ ] Look back at some of your favorite stories from the Old Testament. Identify moments in those passages where you see the theme of God's redemption through Jesus.
- [ ] Continue journaling; write down what God says to you during your prayer time with Him concerning your walk with Him.
- [ ] Other:

WORSHIP

READING PLAN

Read through the following Scripture passages this week. Use the space provided to record your thoughts and responses.

Day 1
John 1:19-31

Day 2
Genesis 3:1-15

Day 3
Exodus 12:21-27

Day 4
Hebrews 9:23-28

Day 5
Hebrews 4:1-11

Day 6
Hebrews 7:22-28

Day 7
Hebrews 10:1-18

DON'T MISS THE FOREST

The saying goes, "Don't miss the forest for the trees." It means that it's entirely possible for us, in any situation, to lose sight of the big picture. We can be so zoomed in on the individual details that we miss the overall theme of what's happening around us.

Jesus' disciples regularly missed the forest throughout His public ministry. They were focused on His miracles and His obvious wisdom. They were also focused on their own expectations that the Messiah would conquer the Roman Empire and re-establish the glory of Israel to its pinnacle in the days of King David and King Solomon.

Consequently, they missed the truth that Jesus had come to offer Himself as a sacrifice. They missed the forest even though Jesus Himself told them His mission:

> 31 Then he took the Twelve aside and told them, "See, we are going up to
> Jerusalem. Everything that is written through the prophets about the Son of
> Man will be accomplished. 32 For he will be handed over to the Gentiles, and he
> will be mocked, insulted, spit on; 33 and after they flog him, they will kill him,
> and he will rise on the third day."
>
> LUKE 18:31-33

Just as it was true for those disciples, we might walk through life and be so focused on the details of what's around us that we miss the fact that God is unfolding His continuing story of redemption. We must widen our scope of vision so that we can see the centrality of Jesus in all things, and align our lives accordingly.

What situations are currently dominating your focus?

How might God be using those circumstances as a part of your continued growth in Christ?

What tends to keep you from seeing God at work in your life and in the world around you? How can a focus on God's Word help you reshape your focus?

PERSONAL STUDY

SHADOWS OF WHAT'S TO COME

We've spent the bulk of this session exploring the truth that Jesus is the central figure in all of Scripture. As part of that exploration, we need to spend some time looking into the Book of Hebrews from the New Testament.

As the name suggests, the Book of Hebrews was originally written to Jewish people who had responded to the gospel message and become disciples of Jesus. Because of persecution and other factors, however, at least some of these Christians were considering a return to their Jewish roots. They were struggling with uncertainty and doubt—perhaps even fear.

In response, the author of Hebrews wrote his letter as a logical, step-by-step argument showing that Jesus is the fulfillment of God's original covenant with His people. He wanted to show that everything God had done and commanded in the Old Testament was designed to lead to Jesus—therefore, Jesus is superior to that covenant and to the Law.

The theme of Jesus' centrality is particularly evident in chapter 10, including this passage:

> [1] Since the law has only a shadow of the good things to come, and not
> the reality itself of those things, it can never perfect the worshipers by
> the same sacrifices they continually offer year after year. [2] Otherwise,
> wouldn't they have stopped being offered, since the worshipers, purified
> once and for all, would no longer have any consciousness of sins? [3] But
> in the sacrifices there is a reminder of sins year after year. [4] For it is
> impossible for the blood of bulls and goats to take away sins.
> HEBREWS 10:1-4

How would you describe the author's primary argument in these verses?

How does that argument connect with Jesus?

Look also at Hebrews 10:5-10. How do those verses point to Jesus?

In the first verse, the author noted that the law represented only a shadow of what was to come. A shadow gives you an impression of whatever is casting it—you know something is there, but you can't make out all the specific features. In the same way, the Old Testament gives us glimpses of Jesus that come into startling clarity when we get to the New Testament.

The practice of animal sacrifice is another example of how Jesus is foreshadowed throughout the Old Testament. The author of Hebrews showed how the system of animal sacrifice, which was supervised by priests, pointed forward to the death and resurrection of Jesus as the ultimate sacrifice for sin:

> 11 Every priest stands day after day ministering and offering the same sacrifices time after time, which can never take away sins. 12 But this man, after offering one sacrifice for sins forever, sat down at the right hand of God. 13 He is now waiting until his enemies are made his footstool. 14 For by one offering he has perfected forever those who are sanctified.
> HEBREWS 10:11-14

The sacrificial system of the Old Testament wasn't "bad"; it was merely incomplete. God always intended for that system to reach its fulfillment through Christ. In other words, there's no need to make sacrifices anymore because Jesus is the best and final sacrifice. There's no need for people in the line of Aaron to serve as high priests because we have the best and final High Priest in Jesus.

Therefore, as Christians, we can rest confidently in the finished work of Jesus on our behalf.

In the Old Testament, the role of the high priest was to intercede between man and God. How does knowing that Jesus is our High Priest change the way we approach God?

How does Jesus' centrality in the Bible help you apply and obey what you find in all portions of the Bible?

JUST ONE HERO

The Bible is very honest with us about the stories it tells. In fact, the Bible goes to great lengths to point out that every so-called hero in the Scriptures also came with flaws:

- David was a man after God's own heart, a great songwriter, and the greatest king over Israel. He was a faithful friend, a tremendous leader, and not bad with a slingshot. He was also a bad father, an adulterer, and a murderer.
- Scripture calls Moses the humblest man who ever lived. He talked with God face to face as a person talks to a person, and he stood in the face of the most powerful man on the planet and boldly proclaimed the word of the Lord. He also killed a man and was prevented from entering the promised land due to his brashness and lack of faith.
- Abraham was the father of God's chosen people, and even when the New Testament was written he was held up as a model of faith. He believed so strongly in God's promises that he did not withhold his only son from the Lord. But he also believed in God so little that he passed his wife off as his sister and allowed her to be taken into another man's harem—all because he was afraid of being killed. Actually, he did that twice.

What's your initial reaction to the people described above?

Take a moment to read Hebrews 11:1-28. What are some flaws represented in the people mentioned there?

Why is it important for us to recognize the flaws and mistakes present in the stories of people in the Bible?

Perhaps one of the reasons why Scripture intentionally points out the flaws of the people within its pages is to help us avoid the mistake of emulating those people. Yes, we should try to demonstrate the kind of courage David showed in his fight against Goliath. Yes, we should aspire to Moses' level of humility and Abraham's level of faith.

But we should never seek to imitate David himself. Nor Moses, nor Abraham. Instead, we should put all our efforts toward emulating Jesus, our Lord and Master, who is the only real Hero in the pages of Scripture.

Imitating the wrong person was as a mistake the people of Jesus' day had made on a grand scale. They loved and revered the stories of the Old Testament in much the same way modern Americans love and revere the founding fathers. Unfortunately, the Israelites of Jesus' day failed to learn from those stories. Worse, they failed to understand how those stories pointed forward to Christ.

Jesus pointed out the gravity of this mistake during a confrontation with the Pharisees:

> 37 The Father who sent me has himself testified about me. You have not
> heard his voice at any time, and you haven't seen his form. 38 You don't
> have his word residing in you, because you don't believe the one he sent.
> 39 You pore over the Scriptures because you think you have eternal life in
> them, and yet they testify about me. 40 But you are not willing to come to
> me so that you may have life. ...
>
> 45 Do not think that I will accuse you to the Father. Your accuser is Moses,
> on whom you have set your hope. 46 For if you believed Moses, you would
> believe me, for he wrote about me. 47 But if you don't believe what he
> wrote, how will you believe my words?
> JOHN 5:37-40,45-47

What steps can you take to make Jesus your primary focus and primary Hero each day?

What opportunities do you have to help others see Jesus as the central Hero throughout the Scriptures?

When we seek to model our lives after another, let's make sure we follow the example Scripture lays out for us. Let's make sure Jesus is our supreme focus—and our only Hero.

SESSION 3

THE GOD WHO SENDS

God sends His message through His people to tell the world of His work for salvation.

GET STARTED

REFLECT

In the previous session, we looked at a passage of Scripture in which Jesus, risen from the dead, showed two disciples the overall story of the Bible. We learned about how we must approach Scripture and life with this overall story of redemption in mind, looking for our place in that story rather than trying to make God fit into ours.

This session, we'll take a deeper look at what it means to serve a God who sends us out. First, take some time to reflect back on what you learned and put into practice over the last several days:

Which of the assignments did you explore this week? How did it go?

What did you learn or experience while reading the Bible?

What questions would you like to ask?

PRAY

Begin this session by connecting with God through prayer. Use the following guidelines as you speak with Him together:

- Confess that Jesus is the center of all things, and ask Him to continue to show you how central He is in your life and in the world around you.

- Pray that this session will help motivate you to join God in His mission of redemption.

- Pray that as you read and study God's Word, you'll gain a greater passion for those who do not yet know Jesus as Savior.

INTRODUCTION

What's the first job you ever had? Was it mowing grass? Working in a fast food restaurant? Maybe working in the family business? Whatever it was, chances are it wasn't your dream job. Unless you're very fortunate, you've probably had many jobs in many places over the course of your lifetime—and you'll probably have many more.

Here's an important truth: those different jobs and roles represent your vocation, but they are not your mission.

Though your vocation changes, your mission never does. Every disciple of Jesus has been given the same mission: to go and make disciples. Regardless of where we go, what our family looks like, what community we live in, or who our employer may be, this mission is static and constant. It must be the driving force that underlies everything else we do.

Unfortunately, most of us think of this mission as secondary to the main parts of life. Rather than underpinning and motivating the other choices we make in life, it's often relegated to something on the side—something we know we ought to be engaged in, yet never truly make time for.

The task is urgent. The command is clear. Our primary work in this world must be making disciples. This is not only the driving force behind our lives, but the underlying motive to everything we do in the church.

Who is someone from your past who discipled you?

What sacrifices did that person make in order help you grow?

In this session, we will look more deeply at the ways in which God has sent us out into the world in order to accomplish His mission. In so doing, we will seek to develop a disciplined and faith-driven approach to this mission so that we can give ourselves fully to the work Jesus has for us.

KNOW THE STORY

The disciples' hopes were crushed. They had left everything to follow Jesus, and for a while they thought their ragtag group of friends might become revolutionaries. It seemed the crowds supporting Jesus were growing thicker by the day, and rumors continued to spread about His teaching and His power.

Then came Judas' betrayal. And the arrest in the Garden of Gethsemane. And the trial. And the crucifixion. The disciples literally watched Jesus die, and they believed their dreams were over.

Thankfully, that wasn't the end of the story! After the resurrection, Jesus miraculously joined His disciples in a locked room. He showed them His hands and His side to verify His identity. Finally, at long last, the disciples rejoiced, for Jesus was alive again. But Jesus didn't join them just to bring them hope; He joined them to send them out.

> 19 When it was evening of that first day of the week, the disciples were gathered together with the doors locked because they feared the Jews. Jesus came, stood among them, and said to them, "Peace be with you."
>
> 20 Having said this, he showed them his hands and his side. So the disciples rejoiced when they saw the Lord.
>
> 21 Jesus said to them again, "Peace to you. As the Father has sent
> me, I also send you." 22 After saying this, he breathed on them
> and said, "Receive the Holy Spirit."
>
> JOHN 20:19-22

How has Jesus' presence brought peace into your life?

How did the Father send Jesus out to accomplish His mission?

What does that say about the ways in which God will send us out to accomplish His mission?

UNPACK THE STORY

SENT WITH INTENTION

God is a sending God. He sent Adam into the garden. He sent Abram into lands unknown. He sent Moses to Pharaoh. He sent the prophets to declare His Word. And He sent Jesus to be born as a baby. Jesus, then, embodies this core characteristic of God not only as the One who is sent, but also as the One who also sends: "Peace to you! As the Father has sent Me, I also send you" (John 20:21).

As disciples of Jesus, we are sent in the same way the Father sent the Son. That means the manner and methodology we take with us in our mission should be the same as that which characterized the mission of Jesus. So, how did the Father send the Son?

First of all, the Father sent the Son with intentionality. Jesus was not sent haphazardly or randomly; instead, He was sent to fulfill the mission of God—which God had established before He set the foundations of the world. Everything Jesus did was intentional and on purpose, right down to the twelve people He intentionally invested in and chose as the future leaders of His church.

Everything Jesus did was intentional and on purpose, right down to the twelve people He intentionally invested in and chose as the future leaders of His church.

What are some examples from the Gospels where we see the intentionality of Jesus' mission?

If we are sent as the Father sent the Son, we must also configure our lives with intentionality. That means we must work, play, set our schedules, and choose our activities all with the aim of accomplishing our work in the world. We must leave intentional time both to be discipled and to make disciples. We must be intentional in our relationships, seeking opportunities for discipleship. We must make sure that everything we do is approached with our primary mission in mind.

When have you felt a strong sense of purpose in your walk with God?

What's a specific area of life that does not feel centered on God's mission?

SENT WITH LOVE

The Father sent the Son with intentionality. He also sent Him with love:

> 16 For God loved the world in this way: He gave his one and only Son, so that everyone who believes in him will not perish but have eternal life. 17 For God did not send his Son into the world to condemn the world, but to save the world through him.
> JOHN 3:16-17

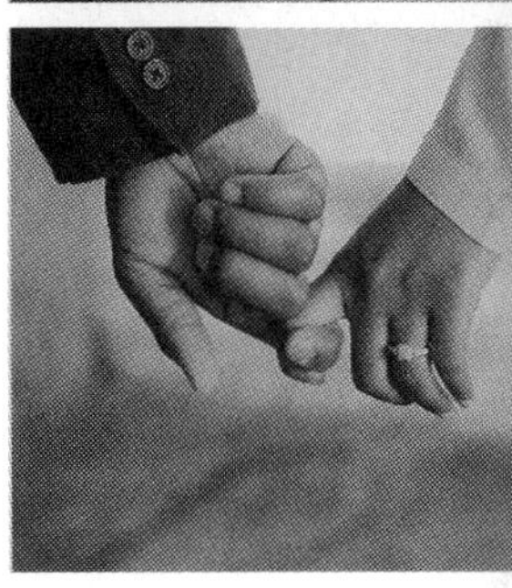

It was out of His great love for the world that God sacrificed His own Son. If we are truly the disciples of Jesus, sent by Him in the same way He was sent by the Father, then our mission must be characterized by this same love.

In love, we must be willing to lovingly tell others the truth about God, the world, sin, and forgiveness. But we must also be willing to bear with others, praying for them, asking the Lord to do His work in their lives. In love, we must persevere in following Jesus and loving those who are difficult to love—including showing grace to those who disagree with us.

What do you find challenging about the principles above?

How should being sent with love influence the way we share the truth with others?

As Jesus' disciples, we also can be absolutely confident of God's love for us.

Jesus knew that He was loved by the Father (see Matt. 3:16-17). And because of that confidence, He was able to work, serve, and even die in freedom. Jesus wasn't constrained by the opinions of others, but being confident in His Father's love, was able to freely give of Himself for the sake of others.

As Jesus' disciples, we also can be absolutely confident of God's love for us. That means we don't have to worry about public opinion or even the circumstances of our lives. We are confident that God loves us completely and will do whatever is best for us. Being confident of this, we are also free to pour ourselves out for the sake of God's mission of making disciples.

ENGAGE

When Jesus came to the mountain after His resurrection, ready to ascend to heaven so that the Holy Spirit might come and empower His disciples and the church in order to complete the Great Commission, He restated that commission with greater specificity:

> [7] He said to them, "It is not for you to know times or periods that the
> Father has set by his own authority. [8] But you will receive power when the
> Holy Spirit has come on you, and you will be my witnesses in Jerusalem, in
> all Judea and Samaria, and to the end of the earth."
>
> ACTS 1:7-8

Spend time as a group thinking about the opportunities for you to carry out God's mission specifically in your community.

Where do you see evidence of urgent needs in your community?

What steps could your church or your group take to help meet those needs?

How can the process of meeting those needs be connected to sharing the gospel?

PRAYER REQUESTS

....

....

....

....

....

....

....

....

In addition to studying God's Word, work with your group leader to create a plan for personal study, worship, and application between now and the next session. Select from the following optional activities to match your personal preferences and available time.

Worship

- [x] Read your Bible. Complete the reading plan on page 42.

- [ ] Spend time with God by engaging the devotional experience on page 43.

Personal Study

- [ ] Read and interact with "Sent to Die" on page 44.

- [ ] Read and interact with "An Old Commission" on page 46.

Application

- [ ] Be intention about showing God's love to someone who needs it this week.

- [ ] Contact a staff person at your church and inquire about the different service projects or community outreach ministries your congregations sponsors. See if there is an opportunity that would be right for you and/or your group.

- [ ] Memorize John 20:21: "Jesus said to them again, 'Peace to you. As the Father has sent Me, I also send you.'"

- [ ] Continue journaling throughout the week, writing down what God speaks to you during your prayer times concerning your mission as His disciple.

- [ ] Other:

READING PLAN

Read through the following Scripture passages this week. Use the space provided to record your thoughts and responses.

Day 1
Genesis 12:1-9

Day 2
Psalm 67:1-7

Day 3
Isaiah 6:1-8

Day 4
Matthew 9:9-38

Day 5
Acts 1:1-8

Day 6
Romans 15:7-21

Day 7
Revelation 7:9-17

A GROUP COMMISSION

We've studied the Great Commission before during the *Disciples Path* journey, but this pivotal passage of Scripture is worth another exploration. While it's true that this commission serves as the foundation for our mission as individual disciples of Jesus, it's also important to note that the Great Commission wasn't given to individuals, but to a group.

Take another look at Jesus' words:

> 18 Jesus came near and said to them, "All authority has been given to me
> in heaven and on earth. 19 Go, therefore, and make disciples of all nations,
> baptizing them in the name of the Father and of the Son and of the Holy Spirit,
> 20 teaching them to observe everything I have commanded you. And remember,
> I am with you always, to the end of the age."
> MATTHEW 28:18-20

As Jesus stood victorious on the hill after His resurrection, He gave this commission to "them"—to all of His followers together. And when Jesus made the promise, "I am with you always," the "you" is plural. This is not a solo mission, but instead a mission to be carried out in the context of community.

As disciples of Jesus, we must not only be committed to this work in the world; we must gather our churches to come alongside us. We do this by engaging one disciple at a time so that the church as a whole is ever-expanding and always moving outward.

How do you respond to the truth that you are not on a solo mission as a disciple of Jesus?

What are some specific ways you've benefited from your relationships with other Christians?

How can you evaluate whether other Christians are benefiting from their relationships with you?

PERSONAL STUDY

SENT TO DIE

We saw in the Group Study portion of this session that Jesus was sent intentionally on God's mission, and that He was sent with love. More than anything else, however, we have to say that Jesus was sent to die. Had Jesus not been crucified, then no matter what else occurred, His ministry on earth would have been a disobedient failure.

It was always the purpose of God that Jesus be crucified and punished for the sin of mankind. This was, and is, the centerpiece of God's plan and His mission for the world.

Of course, if we are Jesus' disciples, and if we are sent as the Father sent the Son, then the inescapable fact is that we are also sent to die:

> 23 Then he said to them all, "If anyone wants to follow after me, let him deny himself, take up his cross daily, and follow me. 24 For whoever wants to save his life will lose it, but whoever loses his life because of me will save it.
> LUKE 9:23-24

What's your initial reaction to this passage? Why?

What does it mean to lose your life as a disciple of Jesus?

Jesus used the metaphor of the cross as an explanation for discipleship. Yet we should remember that during the time when this passage was written, to see someone carrying a cross left no doubt about their future—they were on the road to die.

Jesus wants us to understand that discipleship will require sacrifice. In some cases, it will cost us our literal, physical lives. But in all cases, discipleship will cost us our allegiance.

Disciple are those who have given over control and rule of their lives to another. They no longer hold onto their own hopes, dreams, and aspirations. Instead, they are fully committed to God's will. In our case, God's will is the mission to which He has called us.

How would you assess your willingness to make sacrifices on behalf of God's mission for the world? Consider the following questions based on your life in recent weeks:

To what degree have you been willing to give up your time for the sake of God's mission?

1 2 3 4 5 6 7 8 9 10
Not willing **Very willing**

To what degree have you been willing to give up your money for the sake of God's mission?

1 2 3 4 5 6 7 8 9 10
Not willing **Very willing**

To what degree have you been willing to give up your personal goals and accomplishments at work for the sake of God's mission?

1 2 3 4 5 6 7 8 9 10
Not willing **Very willing**

To what degree have you been willing to give up your relational dislikes and disagreements for the sake of God's mission?

1 2 3 4 5 6 7 8 9 10
Not willing **Very willing**

For Christians in today's cultural and political climate, being disciples who make disciples will cost us time, energy, and resources. It's our daily job as disciples to over and over again remind ourselves that we are fully given over to Jesus.

And it's our daily duty to let that truth dictate the priorities that we follow.

PERSONAL STUDY 2

AN OLD COMMISSION

As we've seen, Jesus' Great Commission in Matthew 28:18-20 is a helpful summary of our mission as His disciples in the world. However, it's important to realize that the main goal behind that commission did not originate after the resurrection. Instead, Jesus was communicating the mission that had been at the heart of God from the very beginning: to create a people set apart for Himself for His own glory, made up of every tribe, tongue, and nation.

For example, if we go back to the moment in the Old Testament when God called Abram to be the father of the Jewish nation, we see shadows of the Great Commission:

> 1 The Lord said to Abram:
>
> > Go out from your land, your relatives, and your father's house to
> > the land that I will show you. 2 I will make you into a great nation,
> > I will bless you, I will make your name great, and you will be a
> > blessing. 3 I will bless those who bless you, I will curse anyone who
> > treats you with contempt, and all the peoples on earth will be
> > blessed through you.
> > GENESIS 12:1-3

Even here, in the first few chapters of the Bible, we see the God who sends people out. Notice, though, the fashion in which Abram was sent. God promised to bless Abram and make him into a great nation. History would prove this to be true, as Abram became Abraham, the father of the Jewish nation. Even more than that, Abraham became the spiritual father of all those who believe in the same God. Jews and Gentiles alike are the spiritual children of Abraham, for they have faith as Abraham did.

Notice also that this blessing wasn't just for Abraham's sake. Instead, Abraham was blessed so that he could be a blessing to others. The same thing is true of his children.

If we believe in Christ, then we are the spiritual children of Abraham. And like him, we've been greatly blessed with the knowledge of Jesus. With this blessing, we too must go out, for we are not merely blessed for our own benefit, but for the sake of others. In other words, we must go, therefore, and preach the gospel to all nations, and in so doing, extend the blessing God has given us to them.

Why is it important to recognize that the Great Commission is also an old commission?

What are some of the dangers of keeping God's blessings to ourselves?

It is God's will for every Christian that we be sent out to do His work in the world. Thankfully, the good we are to do in both word and deed isn't just taking hold of random opportunities. Instead, it's planned beforehand by the wisdom of God:

> [8] For you are saved by grace through faith, and this is not from yourselves;
> it is God's gift— [9] not from works, so that no one can boast. [10] For we
> are his workmanship, created in Christ Jesus for good works, which God
> prepared ahead of time for us to do.
> EPHESIANS 2:8-10

These verses reveal a three-fold component to the Christian life. We are saved: 1) by grace, 2) through faith, and 3) for good works. Not one of these three is negotiable.

Furthermore, Paul helped us know that these good works have been intentionally set out and planned for us ahead of time. It's amazing to consider that, as we walk through our daily lives, God has planned opportunities for us to do His work right in our pathway. These opportunities are there in our workplaces, our homes, and our parties. They're present in our dates, our trips to run errands, and our commutes. God is present and active in our lives; therefore, every day is full of chances to do His work.

The question, then, is not whether the opportunities are there; the question is whether we, as His disciples, will have the faith to see those opportunities and the courage to act on them.

When is a time you remember seeing an opportunity God had put before you to do His work?

What are some practical ways you can be more aware of potential opportunities to do God's work in the world each day?

SESSION 4

GET ON BOARD

Joining God in His mission means letting go of our own hang-ups.

GET STARTED

REFLECT

In session 3, we saw that our God is a sending God. Specifically, He has sent His people out into the world in order to accomplishing His mission for the world—a mission that involves sharing the good news of the gospel, teaching God's Word, and baptizing new disciples through the critical process of discipleship.

Before we move on to take a deeper look at the need to let go of our own prejudices and preconceived opinions in order to join God in that mission, spend some time reflecting back on what you learned and put into practice this week:

Which of the assignments did you explore this week? How did it go?

What did you learn or experience while reading the Bible?

What questions would you like to ask?

PRAY

Begin this session by connecting with God through prayer. Use the following guidelines as you speak with Him together:

- Pray that you would have a greater vision of God's work in the world and your specific place in that work.
- Ask the Lord to continue to grow your passion to be a disciple who makes disciples.
- Praise God for the chance to be a part of His Great Commission. Pray that you will have the courage to release any pride or personal prejudices that may restrict you from joining God in His mission for the world.

INTRODUCTION

Have you ever tried to run away from home? Not in the sense of leaving home at an appropriate time as a college student or young adult, but rather in the sense of packing up a peanut butter sandwich and a few Matchbox cars in your Thomas the Train backpack as a seven-year-old because your parents wouldn't let you have an extra brownie for dessert?

Most of the time such trips are short-lived. But sometimes, if initial argument or circumstance is particularly deep, they may last much longer.

There is no more famous story of running away than that of Jonah. Here was a man so convinced of his own opinion and so opposed to God's direction that he sought to get as far away from the will and reach of God as he could imagine. But this story is less about a man running from God than it's about God's mission to pursue humanity in all of our disobedience.

While Jonah was vindictive, God was merciful. While Jonah was angry, God was forgiving. While Jonah ran away, God pursued—in fact, God pursued both the wicked Ninevites and His own disobedient prophet.

How would you describe your experiences with running away from home?

How would you describe your experiences with running away from God's plan and purpose?

We'll take a deeper look at Jonah's story in this session. Within that story, we'll find a picture of God who is willing to go to great lengths to pursue people even when they have no interest in being found.

We'll also see that, if we want to follow Jesus as His disciples, we cannot hold on to actions or attitudes that are contrary to that mission. We must be joyfully sent out by Jesus on His terms, not our own.

KNOW THE STORY

Jonah was a prophet, meaning his calling was to hear the voice of the Lord and deliver the message to others. The Book of Jonah doesn't represent the first time Jonah heard the word of the Lord. God had used Jonah to declare to the northern kingdom of Israel God's grace and coming blessing (see 2 Kings 14:25).

But this message was different. God wasn't sending Jonah to the Israelites; he was sending him to their foreign enemies the Ninevites. And he was not sending Jonah to declare a message of prosperity, but a message of impending judgment.

What happened next is surprising on many levels:

> [1] The word of the Lord came to Jonah son of Amittai: [2] "Get up!
> Go to the great city of Nineveh and preach against it because
> their evil has come up before me." [3] Jonah got up to flee to
> Tarshish from the Lord's presence. He went down to Joppa
> and found a ship going to Tarshish. He paid the fare and
> went down into it to go with them to Tarshish from the
> Lord's presence.
>
> [4] But the Lord threw a great wind onto the sea, and such a
> great storm arose on the sea that the ship threatened to break
> apart. [5] The sailors were afraid, and each cried out to his god.
> They threw the ship's cargo into the sea to lighten the load.
> Meanwhile, Jonah had gone down to the lowest part of the
> vessel and had stretched out and fallen into a deep sleep.
> JONAH 1:1-5

What are some possible explanations for Jonah's refusal to obey God's command?

When have you felt hesitant to do what you knew God wanted you to do?

UNPACK THE STORY

HEADING IN THE OTHER DIRECTION

Nineveh was to the east of Israel. The Mediterranean Sea, where Jonah set sail, was to the west. So, Jonah literally went in the opposite direction from where God commanded him to go. Why would a prophet make such a choice?

Jonah himself explained his reasoning while talking with God later in the book:

> 2 He prayed to the LORD: "Please, LORD, isn't this what I thought
> while I was still in my own country? That's why I fled toward
> Tarshish in the first place. I knew that you are a gracious and
> compassionate God, slow to anger, abounding in faithful love,
> and one who relents from sending disaster. 3 And now, LORD,
> take my life from me, for it is better for me to die than to live."
> JONAH 4:2-3

Notice it wasn't the character of the Ninevites that made Jonah want to flee; it was the character of the God who sent Him. Jonah wanted no part of bringing God's forgiveness to the people he hated.

Notice it wasn't the character of the Ninevites that made Jonah want to flee; it was the character of the God who sent Him.

What are some situations where Christians today might hold back the gospel from those who need to hear it?

How should disciples of Jesus go about serving those they disagree with—or even those they don't like?

Like Jonah, we know God's character. We know He's quick to forgive, and we know His compassion and grace extend to all who repent. But, like Jonah, we may be more selective in our efforts to share the gospel than we realize. We need to remember that, in the end, our failure to extend the hope of salvation is an unjust judgment.

If we are to live as disciples of Jesus, than we are committed to His mission—both for our lives and for the world. And as we can see in the life of Jonah, God's mission includes pursuing any and all who have turned away from His love.

FORGIVENESS FOR ALL

Moving back to Jonah 1, the prophet could have repented of his disobedience, recommitted to God, and assured the crew that taking him back to shore would calm the storm. Instead, Jonah had himself thrown into the sea.

Even such a supreme act of rebellion did not end God's pursuit. He sent "a great fish" to swallow Jonah as a rescue mission. The end result gave Jonah lots of time to think.

Read Jonah 2:1-10. What strikes you as most interesting about Jonah's prayer? Why?

How has God used discipline in your life to bring you in line with His will?

It's ironic that, while he was in the belly of the great fish, Jonah found himself in the same position as the Ninevites. He was disobedient, living in the middle of God's discipline, and he needed to repent and ask for forgiveness. In a sense, Jonah had to preach the same message to himself that God had instructed him to preach to the Ninevites. And when he applied that message to himself, he was thankful for the same elements of God's character that had driven him to such rage days earlier.

Read Jonah 3:1-5. How do these verses compare and contrast with the opening of Jonah 1?

When we're called to speak the Word of God, we might feel inadequate, afraid, or vulnerable as we do it. But the repentance of the mighty city of Nineveh reminds us that God's Word is living, active, and able to cut all the way to the soul and spirit of humankind (see Heb. 4:12).

As disciples of Jesus, we can share the truth with confidence because of God's power and authority. In fact, the only thing that may stop us from making an impact in the world is allowing our own preferences and prejudices to push us away from God's mission.

The only thing that may stop us from making an impact in the world is allowing our own preferences and prejudices to push us away from God's mission.

ENGAGE

Perhaps the saddest part of Jonah's story is that we don't know how it ended. Did the prophet come to his senses and repent? Did he die up on that hill? Did he return to Israel as a bitter and angry man, never to be used of God again?

Read Jonah 4:1-11. What's emotions do you feel when you read this chapter? Why?

What are some ways we can actively carry out God's mission in our community?

In the broader world?

While Jonah's ending is uncertain, ours is still in process. How will your story end? Will you sit on the hill of disobedience, or will you rejoice in the gracious character of God?

PRAYER REQUESTS

In addition to studying God's Word, work with your group leader to create a plan for personal study, worship, and application between now and the next session. Select from the following optional activities to match your personal preferences and available time.

Worship

- [x] Read your Bible. Complete the reading plan on page 56.
- [ ] Spend time with God by engaging the devotional experience on page 57.

Personal Study

- [ ] Read and interact with "The Angry Prophet" on page 58.
- [ ] Read and interact with "We Go Because We Are Forgiven" on page 60.

Application

- [ ] As you pray throughout this week, ask God's Spirit to convict you of any sinful attitudes or opinions that restrict your ability to participate in His mission. Be sure that you respond to the Spirit's conviction with repentance.
- [ ] During the Engage activity on page 40, your group identified several ways to actively carry out God's mission in your community and in the world. Work as a group to take one of those steps before your next gathering.
- [ ] Memorize Jonah 2:8-9: "Those who cherish worthless idols abandon their faithful love, but as for me, I will sacrifice to you with a voice of thanksgiving. I will fulfill what I have vowed. Salvation belongs to the Lord."
- [ ] Continue journaling throughout the week, writing down what God speaks to you during your prayer times concerning your walk with Him.
- [ ] Other:

WORSHIP

READING PLAN

Read through the following Scripture passages this week. Use the space provided to record your thoughts and responses.

Day 1
Jonah 1:1-17

Day 2
Jonah 2:1-10

Day 3
Jonah 3:1-10

Day 4
Jonah 4:1-11

Day 5
Matthew 18:21-35

Day 6
Acts 2:1-37

Day 7
John 17:9-18

RELUCTANTLY SENT

Jonah was sent to do something by God. But because of his own prejudices, anger, and fears, he refused to go. Jesus, too, has sent us as His disciples into the world:

> 4 While he was with them, he commanded them not to leave Jerusalem, but to
> wait for the Father's promise. "Which," he said, "you have heard me speak about;
> 5 for John baptized with water, but you will be baptized with the Holy Spirit in a
> few days."
>
> 6 So when they had come together, they asked him, "Lord, are you restoring the
> kingdom to Israel at this time?"
>
> 7 He said to them, "It is not for you to know times or periods that the Father
> has set by his own authority. 8 But you will receive power when the Holy Spirit
> has come on you, and you will be my witnesses in Jerusalem, in all Judea and
> Samaria, and to the end of the earth."
>
> ACTS 1:4-8

We are charged with making disciples of all nations (see also Matthew 28:19-20). The question for us is whether we will be held back like Jonah was, or whether we will take up the call of discipleship and go wherever God asks us to go.

How has God's mission for the world influenced your prayer life?

How has God's mission influenced your career plans?

How has God's mission influenced your relationships?

PERSONAL STUDY 1

THE ANGRY PROPHET

As we saw in the Group Study portion of this session, Jonah experienced both conviction and repentance while stuck in the belly of the great fish. However, it seems they didn't fully take hold. Yes, he was faithful in preaching the message God commanded to the people of Nineveh. And yes, his ministry produced some amazing fruit:

> [6] When word reached the king of Nineveh, he got up from his throne, took
> off his royal robe, put on sackcloth, and sat in ashes. [7] Then he issued a
> decree in Nineveh:
>
> By order of the king and his nobles: No person or animal, herd or flock, is
> to taste anything at all. They must not eat or drink water. [8] Furthermore,
> both people and animals must be covered with sackcloth, and everyone
> must call out earnestly to God. Each must turn from his evil ways and
> from his wrongdoing. [9] Who knows? God may turn and relent; he may
> turn from his burning anger so that we will not perish.
>
> [10] God saw their actions—that they had turned from their evil ways—so
> God relented from the disaster he had threatened them with. And he did
> not do it.
>
> JONAH 3:6-10

When have you been convicted to repent of your sin?

You've got to give it to Jonah—he was confident in the power of God's Word and in the gracious character of God Himself. Yet as he watched the Ninevites cry out to God, he was not filled with joy or relief; he was filled with rage.

Read Jonah 4:1-11. What do these verses reveal about Jonah's character?

What do these verses reveal about God's character?

Notice the question God asked Jonah twice during this final chapter: "Is it right for you to be angry?" This is a technique God used several times throughout Scripture when seeking to deal gently with people who needed guidance. For example:

- When Adam and Eve first sinned, God responded with a question: "Where are you?" (Gen. 3:9).
- When Adam and Eve presented themselves, God asked Eve directly, "What is this you have done?" (Gen. 3:13).
- When God responded to Job's accusations, He used a series of questions beginning with, "Where were you when I . . . ?" (Job 38:4).
- When the people said Jesus was a prophet or a reincarnation of John the Baptist, He asked the disciples, "Who do you say that I am?" (Matt. 16:15).

In each of these situations, God wasn't seeking information He didn't already have. Instead, He was gently pressing people into recognizing the true issues of their hearts.

What truth was God highlighting with His questions to Jonah?

If God were to ask you, "Is it right for you to __________________?," what would fill in the blank?

Despite all that had happened in Jonah's life—including the miracle of his rescue in the belly of the great fish—he was still unwilling to confront the deepest corners of his own heart. Like the Ninevites who were clinging to idols, Jonah was clinging to the idol of hatred. He simply couldn't let it go, and his refusal to do so revealed that, though He intellectually recognized the magnitude of God's gracious compassion, he could not put it into practice himself.

Like Jonah, we must confront any long-held prejudice and hatred in our hearts that might cause us to withhold forgiveness and compassion from others. When we bear ill-will toward others, we show that we have not truly understood and experienced the fullness of God's grace given to us.

WE GO BECAUSE WE ARE FORGIVEN

Jesus told a story that relates our own experience of forgiveness to the way we forgive others. When Peter asked a question about how much and how often we must forgive others, Jesus told a story about a servant who'd been forgiven an extravagant debt. Having had his own account settled, he promptly went out and found one of his fellow slaves who owed him a relatively small debt. Instead of extending the same forgiveness he had received, the first servant "grabbed him, started choking him, and said, 'Pay what you owe!'" (Matt. 18:28).

Later, the master heard about what happened. He summoned the slave whose debt he had forgiven:

> 32 Then, after he had summoned him, his master said to him, "You wicked
> servant! I forgave you all that debt because you begged me. 33 Shouldn't
> you also have had mercy on your fellow servant, as I had mercy on you?"
> 34 And because he was angry, his master handed him over to the jailers to
> be tortured until he could pay everything that was owed.
> MATTHEW 18:32-34

Jesus summed up this story by saying: "So also my heavenly Father will do to you unless every one of you forgives his brother or sister from your heart" (v. 35).

What helps you remember the ways God has forgiven you?

Where do you currently have unforgiveness in a relationship?

The truth is Jonah was right about the Ninevites. They deserved to be punished for their wickedness. Jonah, too, deserved to be punished for his disobedience. Even the sailors deserved to be swallowed up by the sea for their idolatry. No doubt there are people in your life and in our culture that deserve the righteous judgment of God—just as we do.

Fortunately, as Jonah knew, God is gracious and compassionate. He loves the people who are in rebellion against Him, which means He loves the people we consider to be our enemies—and He calls us to love them, too. Why? Because sharing the gospel with those who need to hear it is a supreme act of love.

Part of trusting in God is recognizing that as, a perfect Father, God exercises the right discipline toward His children at the right time. Such discipline in our lives is not evidence of God's lack of care; instead, it's proof of His love. As the writer of the Book of Hebrews would later say:

> 7 Endure suffering as discipline: God is dealing with you as sons. For what
> son is there that a father does not discipline? 8 But if you are without
> discipline—which all receive—then you are illegitimate children and
> not sons.
> HEBREWS 12:7-8

Jonah's discipline came in the form of a storm and a great fish. God's discipline of us will probably come in another way. The question is whether we'll recognize and accept His discipline, or whether we'll be angry at His intervention in our lives.

How have you experienced the Lord's discipline in the past?

What is the appropriate way to respond when you think God might be exercising discipline on you?

God loves us too much to allow us to go our own way. He is committed to making sure we take hold of His good and right vision for our lives—and that vision includes the fact that we are sent out into the world to participate in God's mission.

What obstacles have held you back from a greater participation in God's mission for the world?

What's one step you can take to join more fully in God's mission and purpose for your community?

SESSION 5

COMPELLED BY LOVE

The love of Christ motivates us to make disciples.

GET STARTED

REFLECT

In session 4, we saw that disciples of Jesus must let go of their own preferences and prejudices in order to fully participate in God's work for the world. God is committed to using the church to communicate the gospel to all the peoples of the world. He wants us to be a "going" type of people, but we must go on His terms.

In this session, we'll take a deeper look at the way love serves as the foundation for our work in the world on God's behalf. Before we move on, reflect back on what you learned and put into practice over the last week:

Which of the assignments did you explore this week? How did it go?

What did you learn or experience while reading the Bible?

What questions would you like to ask?

PRAY

Begin this session by connecting with God through prayer. Use the following guidelines as you speak with Him together:

- Pray that you would have a greater understanding of Christ's love, both for you and for the world.
- Ask the Lord to continue to grow your passion to be a disciple who makes disciples.
- Praise God for the many ways He has demonstrated His love in your life. Pray that God's love would become your motivation for doing ministry, sharing your faith, and making disciples.

INTRODUCTION

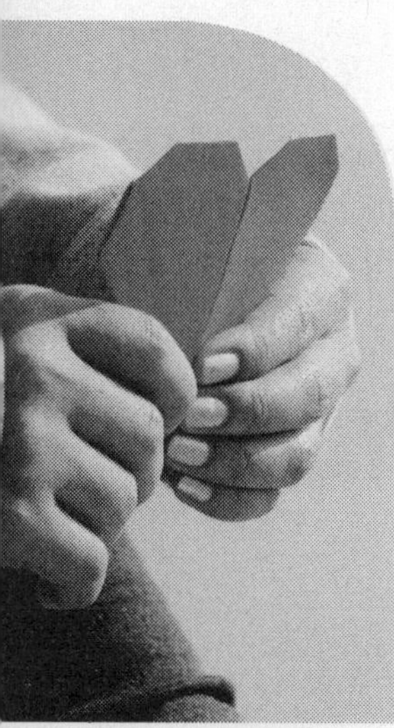

Think about your first childhood crush, or even your "first love." Every time that person walked by, you swooned. Just being around that person gave you a big goofy grin. And when he or she wasn't around, the world seemed a bit more gray.

These are the kinds of people whose love and affection we crave. We want to know their love and we want to love them in return. When we're kids, this is all just puppy-love. It's a childhood infatuation with a person we like. But as we mature, we begin to understand what real love is. The definition begins to take shape in our mind.

Who comes to mind as someone who demonstrates a full and mature love for others?

How has this person (or persons) helped to shape your understanding of what it means to love?

Committing your life to Jesus is more than simple obedience to a set of rules and regulations. It's a commitment of love. We want the highest and best good to occur because of Jesus' work on the earth and in the heavens. And it's through our walk as a believer that we come to know what it is to love Christ.

But consider for a moment that it's not *our* love that begins this relationship. It's Jesus who first loved us—and who first reached out to us. Our faith in Christ is a response to His love toward us.

In this session, we'll take a look at how Christ's love for us is the main and greatest motivation we can find for accomplishing God's work in the world. Through His love for us, we can see how to love others—and we can take action in response to His example.

KNOW THE STORY

In 1 Corinthians 13, the apostle Paul wrote a poignant and powerful message on what love is and how it should impact our lives. You've probably heard that passage quoted numerous times, especially if you've ever been to a wedding.

In his next letter to the church at Corinth, Paul again zeroed in on the topic of love within the church. This time, however, he was more pointed in reminding his readers about the love of Christ—and how that love should motivate us during our walk with Him:

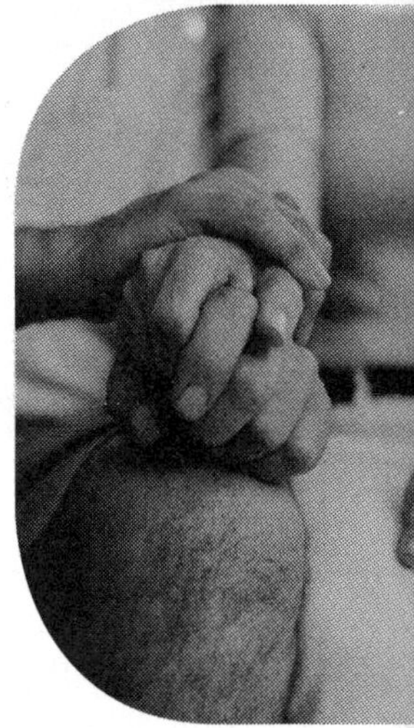

> 11 Therefore, since we know the fear of the Lord, we try to
> persuade people. What we are is plain to God, and I hope it
> is also plain to your consciences. 12 We are not commending
> ourselves to you again, but giving you an opportunity to be
> proud of us, so that you may have a reply for those who take
> pride in outward appearance rather than in the heart. 13 For if
> we are out of our mind, it is for God; if we are in our right mind,
> it is for you. 14 For the love of Christ compels us, since we have
> reached this conclusion: If one died for all, then all died. 15 And
> he died for all so that those who live should no longer live for
> themselves, but for the one who died for them and was raised.
> 2 CORINTHIANS 5:11-15

What do these verses teach about Jesus' love?

What are ways to discuss the implications of Christ's love without becoming "churchy" or superficial?

As you consider this passage of Scripture, remember that the Corinthians were culturally oppressed on every side. Many, if not most, had been rejected by their families for becoming followers of Christ. They also faced persecution from the Roman government and the Jewish authorities in the region.

So what did Paul tell them to do? Find their main motivation in life based on the love of Jesus. That was their best hope, and ours as well.

UNPACK THE STORY

LIVE WITH A NORMAL PASSION

The apostle Paul lived a wheels-off, ready-for-adventure kind of life. His deep belief in Christ's power and love made him appear a little unhinged to some people, which he didn't seem to mind. Focused on being authentic, he wasn't afraid to be seen as out of his mind for the cause of Christ.

But notice the source of Paul's lifestyle: "For the love of Christ compels us…" (v. 14). It wasn't that Paul had independently developed a love for God that drove his spiritual journey. Instead, his entire lifestyle was in response to his experiences with the love of Christ. Because of his encounter with Jesus' love, Paul was pushed to live in a way that reflected that love to others.

The same should be true of us.

What are the actions and attitudes that should define a disciple of Jesus?

What motivates you to demonstrate those actions and attitudes each day?

We need to understand that the kind of life Paul advocated isn't extraordinary or out beyond our reach. It's normal.

We need to understand that the kind of life Paul advocated isn't extraordinary or out beyond our reach. It's normal. We often think of Paul as this radical figure in history, so completely sold out for Jesus that everyone around him thought he was crazy. From a biblical perspective, however, what Paul described in these verses is a normal passion for Jesus. We have sadly lowered our expectations of faithfulness and passion for Jesus to such depths that anything close to Paul's description seems totally unattainable.

In truth, a life that is radically compelled by the love of Christ should be our minimum goal, not the maximum.

We also need to understand that this type of living is in direct opposition to the way of the world. We exist in a me-centric, ego-driven culture—and we find it hard to think about living in any other way. The same was true for the Corinthian Christians. That's why Paul told them again and again that living in response to the love of Christ will always be a counter-cultural experience.

THE LENS OF ETERNITY

When our lives are compelled by the love of Jesus, we don't view people the same way. Paul made that clear in his next argument to the Christians in Corinth:

> 16 From now on, then, we do not know anyone from a worldly
> perspective. Even if we have known Christ from a worldly
> perspective, yet now we no longer know him in this way.
> 17 Therefore, if anyone is in Christ, he is a new creation; the old
> has passed away, and see, the new has come!
> 2 CORINTHIANS 5:16-17

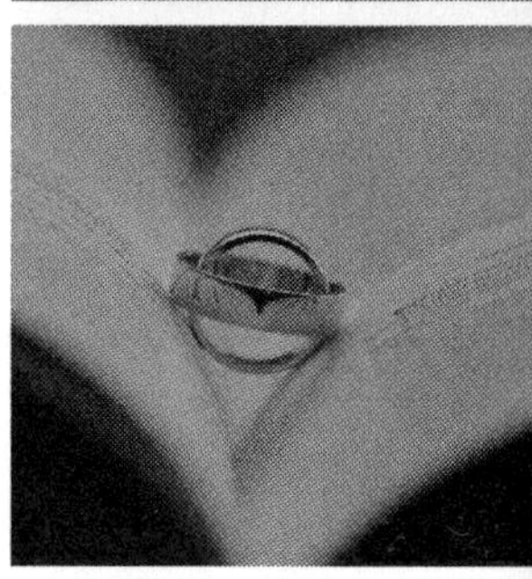

Jesus' love reframes our perspective on everything—and everyone. That's because we see people through the lens of eternity. Normally, our view of people is self-serving. We view others as either interruptions to our day or tools to be used for our happiness. This is the way of the world. The way of Christ is to see others as people with eternal destinies.

C. S. Lewis wrote the following in *The Weight of Glory:* "There are no *ordinary* people. You have never talked to a mere mortal. Nations, cultures, arts, civilisations—these are mortal, and their life is to ours as the life of a gnat. But it is immortals whom we joke with, work with, marry, snub, and exploit."[1]

When do you find it difficult to view people as eternal beings with eternal destinies?

How would adopting this eternal mindset influence the way you see people each day?

Jesus' love reframes our perspective on everything—and everyone.

The love that Christ has shown us also changes how we see Him. Jesus simply cannot be perceived as a nice rabbi who could do mysterious miracles. He was more than a teacher of morality—more than just another spiritual guru with access to higher realms. Like Paul, we must confess that we no longer know Christ in these purely human ways.

We've been given an entirely new life through Christ. Let's honor that gift by viewing the world around us, and the people around us, with His eternal perspective.

ENGAGE

The love of Christ compels both how we live personally toward God and how we interact with others. It should adjust how we view people and how we interact with them. Rather than seeing people as objects to use for the good of our own lives, we see them as individuals who need to know Christ.

Take some time to discuss each of the people groups listed below. Focus your discussion on two questions: 1) How does the world see these people? 2) How should followers of Christ view these people?

- ***The wealthy***
- ***The poor***
- ***Immigrants***
- ***Terrorists***
- ***The unborn***
- ***Children***
- ***Senior citizens***

PRAYER REQUESTS

1. C. S. Lewis, *The Weight of Glory* (New York: Harper Collins, 1980), 46.

WEEKLY ACTIVITIES

In addition to studying God's Word, work with your group leader to create a plan for personal study, worship, and application between now and the next session. Select from the following optional activities to match your personal preferences and available time.

Worship

- [x] Read your Bible. Complete the reading plan on page 70.

- [ ] Spend time with God by engaging the devotional experience on page 71.

Personal Study

- [ ] Read and interact with "A Committed Life" on page 72.

- [ ] Read and interact with "Always Love" on page 74.

Application

- [ ] Memorize 2 Corinthians 5:21: "He made the one who did not know sin to be sin for us, so that in him we might become the righteousness of God."

- [ ] Begin each day with a time of prayer focused on your need to be compelled by Jesus' love. Ask the Holy Spirit to nudge you (or even shove you!) in the direction He wants you to go throughout the day, including taking advantage of opportunities to show radical love to others.

- [ ] Look back at the different types of people listed on page 68. Where do you see these groups represented in your community? What's a step you can take to engage one of those groups in a way that reflects Christ's love?

- [ ] Continue journaling throughout this week. Write down moments when you were especially aware of Christ's love for you.

- [ ] Other:

WORSHIP

READING PLAN

Read through the following Scripture passages this week. Use the space provided to record your thoughts and responses.

Day 1
Mark 12:28-31

Day 2
1 Corinthians 13:1-13

Day 3
1 John 4:7-19

Day 4
Luke 15:11-32

Day 5
Ezekiel 34:11-16

Day 6
Galatians 6:1-5

Day 7
John 16:7-11

A GROUP COMMISSION

Every one of us should be driven with a passionate desire to mirror the love of Christ to the world. Our churches and even our small groups can (and should) participate in this vision. After all, the passages we've studied were written not to individuals, but to the whole church.

When Paul wrote to the Corinthians, he was encouraging a group effort of love. It was to be a church-wide endeavor to be ministers and ambassadors. It's encouraging to live out our faith in this way. We can help each other. We can hold one another's hands when we feel weak. We can celebrate with each other when we see God's victorious love take hold of another person's life.

As Paul wrote to the Corinthians:

> 18 Everything is from God, who has reconciled us to himself through Christ
> and has given us the ministry of reconciliation. 19 That is, in Christ, God was
> reconciling the world to himself, not counting their trespasses against them,
> and he has committed the message of reconciliation to us.
>
> 20 Therefore, we are ambassadors for Christ, since God is making his appeal
> through us. We plead on Christ's behalf: "Be reconciled to God." 21 He made the
> one who did not know sin to be sin for us, so that in him we might become the
> righteousness of God.
> 2 CORINTHIANS 5:18-21

Love is something that must happen in community. How can your group encourage one another to be driven by Christ's love for the world?

What are some practical steps your church can take to express the love of God in your community?

PERSONAL STUDY

A COMMITTED LIFE

We've seen throughout this session that those who've experienced the love of Christ should be changed by the love of Christ. We should be compelled by that love to view our world—and especially our fellow human beings—from an eternal perspective.

Building on this theme, let's remember again that love isn't something God *does;* it's something He *is:*

> 7 Dear friends, let us love one another, because love is from God, and everyone who loves has been born of God and knows God. 8 The one who does not love does not know God, because God is love.
> 1 JOHN 4:7-8

God is love. Therefore, it's inherent to His nature for God to act for the good of His creation. When God sees you, He sees someone that he desires to transform from rebel into family. His love toward you is not merely the sappy puppy-love of adolescents; it's the divine choice that you can be changed by His intervening activity on the cross.

What's the difference between viewing God as a Deity who chooses to love and viewing Him as a Deity who is love?

How does this understanding help you approach God on a daily basis?

Of course, it doesn't do any good for us to have an intellectual understanding of God's nature without allowing that understanding to influence our actions. That's clear as we continue reading through the apostle's message in 1 John:

> 11 Dear friends, if God loved us in this way, we also must love one another.
> 12 No one has ever seen God. If we love one another, God remains in us and his love is made complete in us.
> 1 JOHN 4:11-12

We know we are responding correctly to God's love when it compels us to love one another.

Paul had been changed dramatically by God's love. The entire mission and motivation for his life had been redefined. As he wrote to the Christians in the city of Corinth, he challenged them to join him in embracing that redefinition:

> 17 Therefore, if anyone is in Christ, he is a new creation; the old has
> passed away, and see, the new has come! 18 Everything is from God,
> who has reconciled us to himself through Christ and has given us the
> ministry of reconciliation. 19 That is, in Christ, God was reconciling the
> world to himself, not counting their trespasses against them, and he
> has committed the message of reconciliation to us. 20 Therefore, we are
> ambassadors for Christ, since God is making his appeal through us. We
> plead on Christ's behalf: "Be reconciled to God."
> 2 CORINTHIANS 5:17-20

How have you changed since choosing to follow Christ?

What do these verses teach about our mission and motivation as disciples of Jesus?

When have you felt confident in your mission and motivation as a disciple of Jesus?

Though it will seem odd to the world (and perhaps to some in the church), we are called and commissioned because of Christ's love toward us. You have a message in your hands—the gospel. You have a position to fulfill. You are an ambassador who represents the true King of Glory.

To be God's emissary means that you are committed to "plead on Christ's behalf." Being compelled by the love of Christ begins with redefining your life, and it continues as you let others know that God's love can redefine their lives, as well.

PERSONAL STUDY

ALWAYS LOVE

The idea that love is an overarching theme for our life of faith was not new to Paul, nor was it new to the audience of his letter in 2 Corinthians. In fact, this theme wasn't new to anyone vaguely familiar with the life of Jesus or the Jewish people.

The Israelites had a statement from Deuteronomy 6 that they call the "Shema." It's a foundational statement of faith that summarizes their core beliefs. And at the center of that statement is an expression of love:

> 4 "Listen, Israel: The LORD our God, the LORD is one. 5 Love the LORD your
> God with all your heart, with all your soul, and with all your strength. 6
> These words that I am giving you today are to be in your heart. 7 Repeat
> them to your children. Talk about them when you sit in your house and
> when you walk along the road, when you lie down and when you get up.
> 8 Bind them as a sign on your hand and let them be a symbol on your
> forehead. 9 Write them on the doorposts of your house and on your city
> gates.
> DEUTERONOMY 6:4-9

What do you like best about these verses?

The passage reminds us that loving God isn't something to be done in passing. Rather, it's the defining characteristic of your life. We are called to love the Lord with heart, soul, and strength. As a response to what He's done for us, it should be natural that we would love Him with such a totality of life.

The greater context of the passage instructs faithful people to teach the ways of God to their children and families. But love takes the center stage. Too often, people separate the revelation of God in the Old Testament from the revelation of God in the New Testament. They treat Him like two different beings, or as if He changed His own nature somewhere in the middle of history. In truth, God has always been God. And He has always loved us with the expectation that we will love Him in return.

Where do you see evidence of God's love throughout the Old Testament?

Jesus knew, understood, and lived out the Old Testament. He quoted passages from those Scriptures on numerous occasions, including this interaction with a religious leader:

> [28] One of the scribes approached. When he heard them debating and saw
> that Jesus answered them well, he asked him, "Which command is the
> most important of all?" [29] Jesus answered, "The most important is Listen,
> O Israel! The Lord our God, the Lord is one. [30] Love the Lord your God with
> all your heart, with all your soul, with all your mind, and with all your
> strength. [31] The second is, Love your neighbor as yourself. There is no
> other command greater than these."
> MARK 12:28-31

What do these verses reveal about the need for God's people to demonstrate love?

Who comes to mind when you think of people who demonstrate this kind of love?

Christ emphasized for this man that loving God with the totality of our lives is necessary for us to show ourselves faithful. But He didn't stop there. As religious people, we can be tempted to have an inward focus. We can get satisfied with an "I've got my own stuff with God worked out" attitude.

Jesus, however, wanted to emphasize that our love for God should naturally become a love for others. He went "above and beyond" the scribe's question by providing a second command: to love your neighbor as you would love yourself. In other words, we are to care for those around us like we would care for our own well-being.

Thinking this way will turn your world upside down. Or, perhaps it would be better to say that thinking this way will finally set your world right-side up. As God has loved us, we are to love Him. As we love Him, we are to love others as ambassadors for His kingdom.

No matter how you slice it, love is the centerpiece of the Christian life.

SESSION 6

REVERSING THE CURSE

God will empower His people to make disciples of every nation

GET STARTED

REFLECT

In the previous session, we discovered that the core of disciple-making is the love of Jesus. When we as disciples of Christ have a growing understanding of the depth of love Jesus displayed for us at the cross, we are compelled by that love to extend the message of the gospel to others. Actually, we're compelled not only to share the initial message of the gospel, but to actually carry out Jesus' mission of disciple-making in the world.

In this session, we'll take a deeper look at what it means to have a worldwide perspective on making disciples. Before we move on, reflect back on what you learned and put into practice over the last week:

Which of the assignments did you explore this week? How did it go?

What did you learn or experience while reading the Bible?

What questions would you like to ask?

PRAY

Begin this session by connecting with God through prayer. Use the following guidelines as you speak with Him together:

- Pray for a deeper passion to see Jesus acknowledged as Lord in every part of the world.
- Pray that God would reveal to you any personal biases you might have against specific regions or groups of people.
- Ask the Lord to give you a vision for the way your life can impact the world (and God's kingdom) in an ever-expanding way.

INTRODUCTION

The butterfly effect is a scientific concept that proposes how a single, seemingly insignificant action can have far-reaching effects both now and in the future. The concept gets its name from Edward Lorenz, who believed the details of something as large as a hurricane could be influenced by minor disturbances, such as the flapping wings of a butterfly, several weeks earlier.

Whether in meteorology, science fiction, or life in general, the idea remains the same—no action is so small that it cannot change the world under the right conditions.

What are some ideas or movements throughout history that have literally changed the world?

When have you seen something small or seemingly insignificant have a major impact?

When we take up the Book of Acts, we find a group of disciples who were encouraged by Jesus' resurrection, but still confused and waiting to see what would happen next. To this group, Jesus spoke words of incredible challenge—that these normal people were to carry out a mission with worldwide implications.

Starting in Jerusalem, they were to make disciples of every nation.

This mission would cause these people to confront their fear, apprehension, and personal prejudices. But that's the work God had for His church then, and that's the work God has for His church now. While we, like the early disciples, might be overwhelmed at the idea of reaching the entire world with the message of Jesus, we should be encouraged at the confidence Jesus has placed in His disciples—including us.

Through the power of the Spirit, we can take up this mission starting right where we are, and we can see the gospel go to the far corners of the world.

THE STORY

KNOW THE STORY

How did this happen? That's the question Luke, the author of both the Gospel of Luke and the Book of Acts, was trying to answer in an orderly way. By the time he wrote those two companion volumes, the gospel and the Christian faith had taken the world by storm. What began as a fledgling offshoot of Judaism had sprung roots all over the world. People were following Jesus by the thousands, and they were doing so in all corners of the globe.

After extensive research, Luke wrote down what happened not only that we might know the history, but so that we might also come to see ourselves as active participants in the ongoing mission of God to make disciples of all nations:

> 1 I wrote the first narrative, Theophilus, about all that Jesus began
> to do and teach 2 until the day he was taken up, after he had
> given instructions through the Holy Spirit to the apostles he had
> chosen. 3 After he had suffered, he also presented himself alive
> to them by many convincing proofs, appearing to them over a
> period of forty days and speaking about the kingdom of God.
>
> 4 While he was with them, he commanded them not to leave
> Jerusalem, but to wait for the Father's promise. "Which," he said,
> "you have heard me speak about; 5 for John baptized with water,
> but you will be baptized with the Holy Spirit in a few days."
>
> 6 So when they had come together, they asked him, "Lord, are
> you restoring the kingdom to Israel at this time?"
>
> 7 He said to them, "It is not for you to know times or periods that
> the Father has set by his own authority. 8 But you will receive
> power when the Holy Spirit has come on you, and you will be
> my witnesses in Jerusalem, in all Judea and Samaria, and to the
> end of the earth."
>
> ACTS 1:1-8

What's the most surprising portion of these verses? Why?

Where would you like to see the world change for the better?

UNPACK THE STORY

THE PROMISE OF WITNESS

The Book of Acts is the sequel to the Book of Luke. While we don't know exactly who Theophilus was, it seems from the introductions to both books that this person was Luke's primary audience. Perhaps he was a government official, or maybe a rich patron curious about the spread of this new faith. Either way, Luke wrote these two volumes to explain who Jesus is, and then to clarify how the Holy Spirit empowered Jesus' disciples to continue His work in the world.

As Acts 1 opens, we are dropped into a teaching from Jesus to His first followers. They were still reeling from everything that had just happened, and they wanted to know what Jesus' resurrection meant for them and for the world. But Jesus wasn't interested in educating them; He was more concerned with giving them a command and a promise.

Acts 1:8 serves both functions. It's a command in the same way that the Great Commission (Matthew 28:18-20) is a command—that disciples of Jesus are to go and make more disciples. But it's also a promise in that Jesus said those same followers *will be* His witnesses to the end of the earth.

What God promises, He fulfills. For His disciples today, that means there's no more certain cause we can give ourselves to than God's mission of worldwide discipleship.

How does the command present in Acts 1:8 apply to modern followers of Jesus?

How does the promise present in Acts 1:8 apply to us?

Throughout the Book of Acts, we see God keeping this promise both through the voluntary and involuntary means of His disciples. We see the voluntary missionary journeys of people like Paul, but we also see the scattering of the disciples to all corners of the world through persecution (see Acts 8:1). Each moment recorded in the journey of the early church show just how serious God is about His mission being fulfilled.

What God promises, He fulfills. For His disciples today, that means there's no more certain cause we can give ourselves to than God's mission of worldwide discipleship. This cause *will* be completed—not because of our strength, ingenuity, or courage, but because God has promised through His Son that it would be so.

THE EXPANSION OF WITNESS

Jesus promised that we would be His witnesses. But He also said His witnesses would move outward in ever-expanding circles. Look again at His words:

> But you will receive power when the Holy Spirit has come on you, and you will be my witnesses in Jerusalem, in all Judea and Samaria, and to the end of the earth.
> ACTS 1:8

Each of these places gets larger and larger in area, starting with a city and then moving into a territory and then into a region. So, the witness of the disciples was meant to go further and further out. But the expansion of the gospel wasn't merely geographical; it was also meant to be cultural.

Jerusalem was relatively comfortable for the early disciples. True enough, this was the city where Jesus was crucified, but it was also the center of Judaism and religious culture. These were the people, the customs, the language, and the beliefs with which the disciples were most familiar.

But being witnesses for Jesus requires the crossing of those boundaries of familiarity and comfort. The early disciples were also called to places like Samaria, where they would speak the good news to people generally considered (by the Jews) to be unworthy of association. Beyond that, they would go even to the furthest reaches of the Gentile world. The conclusion was clear—this gospel was for all people.

The expansion of the gospel wasn't merely geographical; it was also meant to be cultural.

In order to embrace this mission, the early Christians needed to confront their own biases. They needed to acknowledge that all people—regardless of race, background, or condition—stand as condemned sinners in equal need of the gospel. We must do the same.

To what degree do you regularly associate with people who are not like you?

Where do you see opportunities for your group (or your church) to expand its witness for Jesus?

ENGAGE

It's apparent that the early disciples needed Jesus' command to think globally about their mission to make disciples. Look again at verse 6: "So when they had come together, they asked him, 'Lord, are you restoring the kingdom to Israel at this time?'" They were still concerned about their old dreams of the Israelite nation rising to power and throwing off the shackles of Rome.

Christians today can also be inwardly focused when it comes to participating in God's kingdom, and there's one area in particular where we often fall short of a global worldview: prayer. If we are truly called to join God in His mission for the world, then we should pray worldwide prayers.

Spend time as a group praying for different parts of the world. Use the following questions as guidelines for your prayer, and remember that the purpose of your prayer is not to solve the problems you address, but rather ask that God would accomplish His will.

What are some major needs that exist in countries other than your own?

Where is the gospel flourishing in countries other than your own?

Where is the gospel being suppressed or opposed?

PRAYER REQUESTS

In addition to studying God's Word, work with your group leader to create a plan for personal study, worship, and application between now and the next session. Select from the following optional activities to match your personal preferences and available time.

Worship

- [x] Read your Bible. Complete the reading plan on page 84.
- [ ] Spend time with God by engaging the devotional experience on page 85.

Personal Study

- [ ] Read and interact with "Witness Defined" on page 86.
- [ ] Read and interact with "Breaking Down the Walls" on page 88.

Application

- [ ] Memorize Acts 1:8: "But you will receive power when the Holy Spirit has come on you, and you will be my witnesses in Jerusalem, in all Judea and Samaria, and to the end of the earth."
- [ ] Continue praying global prayers throughout this week. Consider praying that God's mission will be accomplished in a different region or country each day.
- [ ] Find a restaurant or coffee shop in your community that lets you connect with people who are different from you—different in terms of their ethnicity, beliefs, finances, politics, and so on.
- [ ] Continue journaling, writing down what God speaks to you during your prayer time with Him concerning your walk with Him.
- [ ] Other:

READING PLAN

Read through the following Scripture passages this week. Use the space provided to record your thoughts and responses.

Day 1
Isaiah 42:1-9

Day 2
Isaiah 42:10-17

Day 3
Ephesians 2:11-22

Day 4
Acts 13:13-41

Day 5
Acts 13:42-52

Day 6
Acts 15:1-21

Day 7
Acts 15:22-41

FAMOUS LAST WORDS

What would you communicate to those closest to you if you knew it was the last thing they would hear you say? No doubt you would consider those words carefully to make sure they imparted not only great meaning and wisdom, but also some manner of hope regarding the way you'd want them to carry on without you.

That's exactly what we have in the first chapter of Acts. Jesus, the Son of God and the King of the Universe, gave the command to be witnesses to the end of the earth as His departing words before the coming of the Holy Spirit. Out of all the things He could have communicated at this time, He chose that specific mission; therefore, it should still be ringing in our ears today.

Look at Jesus' words one more time:

> [7] He said to them, "It is not for you to know times or periods that the Father
> has set by his own authority. [8] But you will receive power when the Holy Spirit
> has come on you, and you will be my witnesses in Jerusalem, in all Judea and Samaria, and to the end of the earth."
>
> ACTS 1:1-8

What obstacles have hindered you from maintaining a global focus on God's mission in the past?

What obstacles might be hindering you now?

How can you move one step closer to a full participation in Jesus' mission for all nations and all people?

God is commanding our participation as witnesses to the end of the world. Such a focus is not an option if we are His disciples; it's a matter of obedience to the One who gave the command.

PERSONAL STUDY

WITNESS DEFINED

We've mentioned several times in this session that God has called us to be His witnesses. But that begs an important question: what is a "witness"? Or, what does it mean to serve as a witness within God's kingdom? Obviously, these are questions we need to answer if we truly seek to live inside of the mission and promises of Jesus.

Thankfully, we can find some answers back in Acts 1. For example:

> After he had suffered, he also presented himself alive to them by many convincing proofs, appearing to them over a period of forty days and speaking about the kingdom of God.
> ACTS 1:3

For 40 days after His resurrection, Jesus had been both appearing to and teaching His disciples in Jerusalem. Though they might not have recognized it at the time, Jesus was bolstering the content of their witness.

Fundamentally, the word "witness" is related to giving testimony. In a legal sense, a witness is meant to give either an eyewitness account of what they themselves have experienced, or else to provide an expert opinion. In fact, if a witness is led to speak about events they have not directly experienced themselves, a judge will rule that part of their testimony to be inadmissible.

So, the primary role of the apostles in the Book of Acts was simply to recount their experiences as eyewitnesses of the life, death, and resurrection of Jesus Christ.

Why would such an account (or such witnesses) be important for the early days of the church?

As present-day witnesses and followers of Christ, to what events are we expected to give testimony?

While we have not physically put our hands in the holes in Jesus' hands or shared a physical meal with Him in His resurrected state, we are nonetheless witnesses today. But as witnesses, we must also feel the same kind of constraint to our testimony that these early apostles did. Meaning, we are meant to testify about that which we have experienced.

What have we experienced? We've experienced being rescued from our sin. We've experienced the power of the Holy Spirit. We've experience the ways in which Jesus is conforming us to His image day by day, and a host of other things. But all these experiences center on the reality of the living Christ. That is the core of our message—not ourselves, not our abilities, and not our winning personalities. We bear witness to Jesus and what He has done and is doing in our lives.

What specific experiences come to your mind when you read the above paragraph?

Here's a final thought: witnesses must be prepared in order to give proper testimony. We do ourselves a disservice—and we do our Lord a disservice—when our strategy for witnessing to others about the truth of the gospel comes down to "winging it" and hoping the message gets across.

Remember this command from the apostle Peter:

> 14 But even if you should suffer for righteousness, you are blessed. Do not
> fear what they fear or be intimidated, 15 but in your hearts regard Christ
> the Lord as holy, ready at any time to give a defense to anyone who asks
> you for a reason for the hope that is in you.
> 1 PETER 3:14-15

Do you feel prepared to serve as an effective witness for Christ?

What steps would you like to take to become more prepared?

PERSONAL STUDY

BREAKING DOWN THE WALLS

There are many reasons we know the gospel is true. We know it's true because of the fruit in our own lives, for example—the outworking of the Holy Spirit in tangible ways among us. We know it's true because of historical validation and eyewitness accounts. We know it's true because of the way, not only in the Bible but before our very eyes, that people change in a moment when they encounter Jesus.

But in the New Testament, perhaps the main validation of the reality of the power of the gospel isn't what you'd think of at first glance. In the Book of Ephesians, for example, the primary apologetic for the gospel is the church itself. Specifically, Paul emphasized the racial diversity of God's people:

> 11 So then, remember that at one time you were Gentiles in the flesh—
> called "the uncircumcised" by those called "the circumcised," which is
> done in the flesh by human hands. 12 At that time you were without Christ,
> excluded from the citizenship of Israel, and foreigners to the covenants
> of promise, without hope and without God in the world. 13 But now in
> Christ Jesus, you who were far away have been brought near by the blood
> of Christ. 14 For he is our peace, who made both groups one and tore down
> the dividing wall of hostility.
> EPHESIANS 2:11-14

What do you like best about these verses? Why?

The church at Ephesus was a racially diverse congregation where Jews and Greeks worshiped alongside one another. In his letter to the Ephesians, Paul emphasized the necessity of maintaining and celebrating that togetherness—of working to become a single, unified congregation. That's not to say the Ephesians didn't have their troubles; they certainly did. But they were together under one Head, which was Christ. And that togetherness was an extremely convincing evidence for the truth of the gospel.

Look around the church today, and there are still walls. Still hostility. Still division. And so the call to tear down that which Jesus has already torn down continues to resound.

Where have you seen unity and diversity within the church?

As we look at the church in the New Testament, we can't help but be reminded of a well-known (but often ignored) moment from the very beginning of God's Word: the Tower of Babel.

Read about the Tower of Babel in Genesis 11:1-9. How would you summarize the main point or purpose of that story?

The people described in this story weren't simply interested in building a tower. Instead, they were seeking to throw off the glory of God in favor of making a name for themselves. They were boldly declaring their independence from their Creator and rejecting His authority over their lives. God's judgment for this act of defiance was to confuse their language and scatter them across the world.

Centuries later in the Book of Acts, we see God using His disciples to reverse the curse of Babel. We see that in Acts 1:8, where Jesus sent His disciples to be His witnesses "in Jerusalem, in all Judea and Samaria, and to the end of the earth." And we see the ultimate reversal of the Babel curse in this picture of Christ's bride, the church, in the Book of Revelation:

> 9 After this I looked, and there was a vast multitude from every nation, tribe,
> people, and language, which no one could number, standing before the throne and
> before the Lamb. They were clothed in white robes with palm branches in their
> hands. 10 And they cried out in a loud voice: "Salvation belongs to our God, who is
> seated on the throne, and to the Lamb!"
> REVELATION 7:9-10

God's desire is for all people who've been scattered because of their disobedience to return to one, new people in Christ—working together for His kingdom and speaking together the common language of grace. As disciples of Jesus in the 21st century, we have a tremendous opportunity to give ourselves to this great and eternal work.

What are some active steps you can take in your personal life to help foster a greater unity in the body of Christ?

SESSION 7

LIVING BY THE SPIRIT'S POWER

The Holy Spirit inside us empowers us to speak and live God's message to the world

GET STARTED

REFLECT

In session 6, we examined the call to global discipleship. We saw that God intends for disciples of Jesus not to stay within the confines of the comfortable and familiar, but instead be moving ever outward to the very end of the world. We also saw that our willingness to bridge the gap between nations and cultures with the gospel is a powerful testimony to what Jesus has done for us personally, and reveals how deeply the message of the gospel has taken root in us.

In this session, we'll see how the Holy Spirit fuels and empowers that movement, both in the church and in our personal lives. Before we move forward, reflect back on what you learned and put into practice over the past week:

Which of the assignments did you explore this week? How did it go?

What did you learn or experience while reading the Bible?

What questions would you like to ask?

PRAY

Begin this session by connecting with God through prayer. Use the following guidelines as you speak with Him together:

- Pray that God would help you have a greater understanding of and appreciation for the work of the Holy Spirit.
- Ask God to help you more fully experience the power that comes with living according to the Spirit.
- Pray that God would use this study to give you courage to engage in His mission.

INTRODUCTION

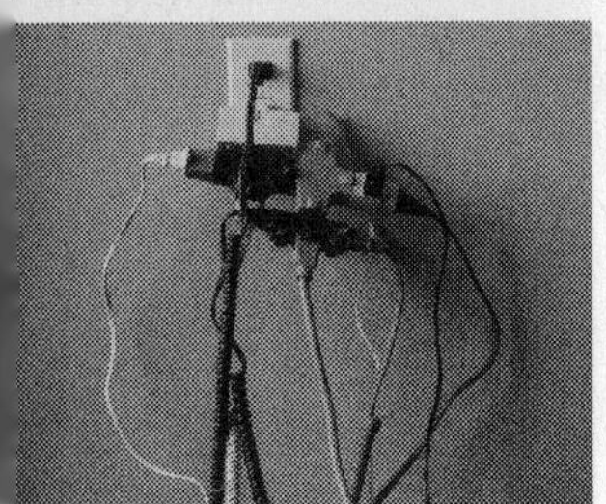

Power is necessary for daily life. Most everything we do requires power. Turn on the lights? You need power. Drive to work? You need power. Take another breath? You need power. This power comes from all kinds of sources—the electric company, gasoline, food—depending on the mechanism that's being powered.

For the most part, those power sources don't really care how the power they provide is used. For example, you have several electrical outlets in your home. The power within those outlets is made available to you by the electric company, but the electric company has no way of monitoring what you use that power to accomplish. They monitor how much power you consume, of course, but they really don't care what you do with it.

For Christians, the Holy Spirit provides the power for our spiritual lives. But the Holy Spirit isn't like the electric company; the Spirit doesn't exist simply to provide power without caring how that power is used. Instead, God the Holy Spirit cares a great deal about how that power is exercised. Namely, we have His power given to us for the accomplishment of God's mission.

When we align ourselves with God's mission, we will find—just as the early disciples did—that the Holy Spirit is more than willing and able to give us all the power we need.

What ideas or images come to mind when you think of the Holy Spirit?

Do you feel powerful as a Christian? Explain.

In this session, we'll take another look at the Holy Spirit's dramatic arrival on the early church, as well as the effects of the Spirit's power within that early community of believers and beyond. In doing so, we'll discover again how the Spirit enabled those Christians to live out the mission God had for them—and how that same Spirit wants to empower us in similar ways.

THE STORY

KNOW THE STORY

After Jesus' resurrection, He commanded His disciples not to leave Jerusalem, but to wait for the Father's promise (see Acts 1:4). So they waited. They likely had no idea what was going on, but they obeyed. And then it happened:

> 1 When the day of Pentecost had arrived, they were all together
> in one place. 2 Suddenly a sound like that of a violent rushing
> wind came from heaven, and it filled the whole house where
> they were staying. 3 They saw tongues like flames of fire that
> separated and rested on each one of them. 4 Then they were
> all filled with the Holy Spirit and began to speak in different
> tongues, as the Spirit enabled them.
> ACTS 2:1-4

The effects of this moment were immediate and dramatic. These ordinary, unschooled tradesmen began to speak in different languages. The gospel was proclaimed first by Peter (see vv. 14-36), then by all the disciples—and the results were amazing:

> 42 They devoted themselves to the apostles' teaching, to the
> fellowship, to the breaking of bread, and to prayer. 43 Everyone
> was filled with awe, and many wonders and signs were being
> performed through the apostles. 44 Now all the believers were
> together and held all things in common. 45 They sold their
> possessions and property and distributed the proceeds to all, as
> any had need. 46 Every day they devoted themselves to meeting
> together in the temple, and broke bread from house to house.
> They ate their food with joyful and sincere hearts, 47 praising
> God and enjoying the favor of all the people. Every day the Lord
> added to their number those who were being saved.
> ACTS 2:42-47

Where do you see the Spirit's power evident in these verses?

What are your hopes for being empowered by the Spirit?

UNPACK THE STORY

THE SPIRIT OF GOD

There are some people, both past and present, who believe not in God as the Trinity, but instead that God has only existed as a different person of that Trinity at different points in history. So, in the beginning, there was the Father. And then at Bethlehem, God became the Son. Then here, in Acts 2, God became the Holy Spirit.

This is not so. The Trinity is mysterious, but it's also a foundational reality in the universe. For all eternity, God has existed in perfect fellowship with Himself in three Persons—Father, Son, and Spirit. Three Persons, one God.

In other words, we don't find a new spirit in Acts 2. But we do find a new way in which the Holy Spirit works in the world.

Think back to the scene in that upper room. There was the mighty sound. Then the fire. But notice how the fire was distributed: it came and rested on each person present. This is what happens to every Christian when they're born again. It happens whether you're young or old, whether you're rich or poor, whether you're educated or uneducated, whether you're from Middle Tennessee or Western Africa. The Holy Spirit of God comes to dwell inside of us individually.

Even Jesus Himself said it was for His followers' benefit that He went away so that the Spirit would come (see John 16:7).

That is an astounding thing! It's astoundingly good news. Even Jesus Himself said it was for His followers' benefit that He went away so that the Spirit would come (see John 16:7).

How often do you think about the Holy Spirit? Do you think about Him more or less than the Father or the Son? Why?

What are some specific ways you seek to access the Spirit's power in your life?

As Christians, the Holy Spirit doesn't fill us and empower us solely for our benefit; He specifically fills us so that we might be empowered to live out the mission of God, just as these early disciples did. We aren't meant to simply soak up the blessings of having God live in and through us; we're meant to be a conduit for that power and those blessings to accomplish God's work all the way to the end of the earth.

THE PEOPLE OF GOD

This account teaches us about the Spirit of God, but it also teaches us about the people of God. It shouldn't be lost on us that these disciples gathered in the upper room were the same ones who consistently misunderstood the purposes of Jesus. They were the ones who never grasped His true nature and true mission. They were the ones who scattered and denied Him during His trial and crucifixion. They were the ones who, after the resurrection, were full of doubt and fear. They were uneducated, unschooled, afraid, timid, regular people. Even the crowd, after the disciples spilled out of the house, couldn't believe what they were seeing because they knew these were just regular old Galileans (see Acts 2:7).

In other words, the early disciples were pretty much the same as us.

We are, if nothing else, ordinary. We have ordinary cars, ordinary jobs, and ordinary responsibilities. We change ordinary diapers, pay ordinary taxes, and eat ordinary dinners.

In what ways do you feel ordinary?

How can your "ordinariness" help your work in accomplishing God's mission?

Yes, we're ordinary people. But that's not all. Because of the gospel, we're also children of God. We're co-heirs with Jesus. We're the recipients of an eternal inheritance. We're the dearly loved and treasured objects of God's grace.

Because of the gospel, we're also children of God. We're co-heirs with Jesus.

This is one of the most incredible ironies of the universe—that God has entrusted the message of His wonders to the likes of us. But He has. We're the ones who bear witness to the wonders of God. This is our stewardship in the world.

Read 2 Corinthians 4:4-7. How do these verses contribute to your understanding of yourself as a "person of God"?

ENGAGE

What stands in the way of our experiencing the Spirit's power? Many things. But perhaps chiefly among those obstacles is our preoccupation with our own desires. If we want to see the kind of life the Holy Spirit wants for us—and the kind of power He wants to give to us—we must be willing, as Jesus said, to daily die to ourselves (see Luke 9:23).

Spend time as a group discussing—and perhaps even confessing—specific obstacles that have prevented you from being fully empowered by God's Spirit. Use the following questions as a guide:

What are general obstacles or routines that have hindered your experiences with the Holy Spirit?

What are specific desires that have overshadowed or detracted from your experiences with the Spirit?

What are some practical ways you can surrender to the Spirit each day?

PRAYER REQUESTS

In addition to studying God's Word, work with your group leader to create a plan for personal study, worship, and application between now and the next session. Select from the following optional activities to match your personal preferences and available time.

Worship

- [x] Read your Bible. Complete the reading plan on page 98.
- [ ] Spend time with God by engaging the devotional experience on page 99.

Personal Study

- [ ] Read and interact with "Be Filled" on page 100.
- [ ] Read and interact with "Spirit-Filled Community" on page 102.

Application

- [ ] Memorize Acts 2:42: "They devoted themselves to the apostles' teaching, to the fellowship, to the breaking of bread, and to prayer."
- [ ] Commit to removing something from your regular daily routine—something you spend time doing, watching, reading, and so on most days. Use that time to pray, instead, seeking to get on board with the Holy Spirit's agenda.
- [ ] Talk to a staff person or leader at your church to identify ministries in which the Holy Spirit is at work. See if there is an opportunity for you to join the Spirit's work in a way that allows you to use your gifts.
- [ ] Continue journaling throughout the week. Be intentional about recording moments when you feel a deeper connection with God's Spirit.
- [ ] Other:

READING PLAN

Read through the following Scripture passages this week. Use the space provided to record your thoughts and responses.

Day 1
Joel 2:18-32

Day 2
Ezekiel 36:22-30

Day 3
John 16:5-15

Day 4
Acts 2:1-40

Day 5
Acts 2:41-47

Day 6
1 Corinthians 1:18-31

Day 7
2 Corinthians 4:7-18

BE AWARE

What can we take from this account of the Holy Spirit's power in Acts 2? At least in part, it's this: the people of God are empowered by the Spirit of God to live in the mission of God. As God's people, we must be confident as we live and move throughout our days—not because we have all the answers or the strategy for making disciples, but because of the Spirit at work in and through us.

But we must also have a posture of awareness. We must constantly be looking for where God, through the Spirit, is already at work. And then we must seek to join Him there. Once we begin to live with this kind of awareness, we'll find that the Holy Spirit is busy working in the people around us each and every day. And we'll find that God seeks to use us as His instruments in their lives.

Philip gave us a great picture of that kind of awareness in the early days of the church:

> 26 An angel of the Lord spoke to Philip: "Get up and go south to the road that
> goes down from Jerusalem to Gaza." (This is the desert road.) 27 So he got up
> and went. There was an Ethiopian man, a eunuch and high official of Candace,
> queen of the Ethiopians, who was in charge of her entire treasury. He had
> come to worship in Jerusalem 28 and was sitting in his chariot on his way home,
> reading the prophet Isaiah aloud.
>
> 29 The Spirit told Philip, "Go and join that chariot."
>
> 30 When Philip ran up to it, he heard him reading the prophet Isaiah, and said,
> "Do you understand what you're reading?"
>
> 31 "How can I," he said, "unless someone guides me?" So he invited Philip to
> come up and sit with him.
>
> ACTS 8:26-31

What do you like best about this passage? Why?

Read the rest of the story in Acts 8:32-40. What were the results of Philip's awareness of the Holy Spirit's work around him?

BE FILLED

The Book of Ephesians is filled with lots of great advice for disciples of Jesus. But there's an especially interesting command in this passage that is worth our attention:

> 15 Pay careful attention, then, to how you live—not as unwise people but
> as wise— 16 making the most of the time, because the days are evil. 17 So
> don't be foolish, but understand what the Lord's will is. 18 And don't get
> drunk with wine, which leads to reckless living, but be filled by the Spirit:
> 19 speaking to one another in psalms, hymns, and spiritual songs, singing
> and making music with your heart to the Lord, 20 giving thanks always
> for everything to God the Father in the name of our Lord Jesus Christ,
> 21 submitting to one another in the fear of Christ.
> EPHESIANS 5:15-21

What emotions do you experience when you read these verses?

What are the commands present in these verses?

Which of those commands are especially relevant in your life?

Look at the last part of verse 18: "be filled by the Spirit." This is a pivotal command for any Christian who desires to live out God's will for his or her life. Interestingly, while that clause is indeed a command, indicating that we as Christians have a part to play in being filled with the Spirit, it's also written in the passive voice. In case you need to brush up on your grammar, the active voice is what you see when you're supposed to actively do something, while the passive voice is used when something is done to you. It's the difference between "Kill that spider" and "Spider, be killed."

So, what we find in Ephesians 5:18 is a biblical command that's supposed to be done to us. How does that even happen?

The lesson is that we don't fill ourselves with the Holy Spirit. But we do make ourselves available to be filled by the Spirit. We can choose obedience in the little things of life. We can spend time meditating on the Word of God. We can practice the spiritual disciplines. We can pray. We can fast. We can do all of these things and more—and when we do, we're putting ourselves in a posture of surrender to God. He takes care of it from there.

What are some "little things" that are going well in your spiritual life?

What are some "little things" that need some work?

Being filled with the Spirit is really about yielding control. We set the conditions, trust in the Spirit of Jesus, and surrender. Yield. Stop. That's why in Ephesians 5 the filling of the Spirit is linked, though oppositely, to drunkenness: "So don't be foolish, but understand what the Lord's will is. And don't get drunk with wine, which leads to reckless living, but be filled by the Spirit" (Ephesians 5:17-18).

In the same way that abusing alcohol can impair one's judgment, being filled with the Spirit takes us out of the driver's seat and yields the direction of our lives to Him. That is God's will for your life.

How well do you understand what it means to be filled by the Spirit?

1 2 3 4 5 6 7 8 9 10

None Fully understand

To what degree have you yielded control of your life to God through His Holy Spirit?

1 2 3 4 5 6 7 8 9 10

None Fully understand

What questions would you like answered about being filled by the Spirit?

PERSONAL STUDY 2

SPIRIT-FILLED COMMUNITY

As you look back at Acts 2, you'll notice that one of the effects of the filling of the Holy Spirit was a unique kind of Christian community:

> 42 They devoted themselves to the apostles' teaching, to the fellowship,
> to the breaking of bread, and to prayer. 43 Everyone was filled with awe,
> and many wonders and signs were being performed through the apostles.
> 44 Now all the believers were together and held all things in common.
> 45 They sold their possessions and property and distributed the proceeds
> to all, as any had need. 46 Every day they devoted themselves to meeting
> together in the temple, and broke bread from house to house. They ate
> their food with joyful and sincere hearts, 47 praising God and enjoying the
> favor of all the people. Every day the Lord added to their number those
> who were being saved.
> ACTS 2:42-47

We can see the same emphasis on Christian community as an effect of the Holy Spirit's work in the Book of Philippians:

> 1 If then there is any encouragement in Christ, if any consolation of love,
> if any fellowship with the Spirit, if any affection and mercy, 2 make my joy
> complete by thinking the same way, having the same love, united in spirit,
> intent on one purpose. 3 Do nothing out of selfish ambition or conceit, but
> in humility consider others as more important than yourselves. 4 Everyone
> should look out not only for his own interests, but also for the interests
> of others.
> PHILIPPIANS 2:1-4

What are some themes or truths that overlap in these two passages?

What are some actions or attitudes that overlap?

One of the themes that's evident in these passages is the importance of unity. In fact, when disciples of Jesus are filled and empowered by the Holy Spirit, one of the most tangible evidences of that posture of surrender to the work and will of God is their Christian unity. That's because Jesus doesn't only bring reconciliation between people and God. Through the ongoing work of His Holy Spirit, He also brings reconciliation between people and people within God's kingdom.

For this reason, relational strife is one of the great hindrances to our living in the power of the Spirit. When we hold things against one another, when we refuse to extend grace and forgiveness, when we are unwilling to repent for our sin both to God and to each other—we quench the work of the Spirit in and through the church.

Look at Paul's appeal to the early Christians in the city of Corinth, for example:

> Now I urge you, brothers and sisters, in the name of our Lord Jesus Christ, that all of you agree in what you say, that there be no divisions among you, and that you be united with the same understanding and the same conviction.
> 1 CORINTHIANS 1:10

Though we might look for something more mystical to be connected with the filling of the Spirit, we'd do well to start here with relational unity. Consider whether disunity in the body of Christ is setting up a barrier for us to experience everything God wills for us in Christ. Actually, let's not only consider it—let's do the God-honoring work of reconciliation with one other so that we might see the kind of love and unity God desires in His family.

How have you been affected by relational strife in recent years?

How has that strife affected your connection with God's Spirit?

What are some steps you can take to help contribute to unity within your congregation? Your community?

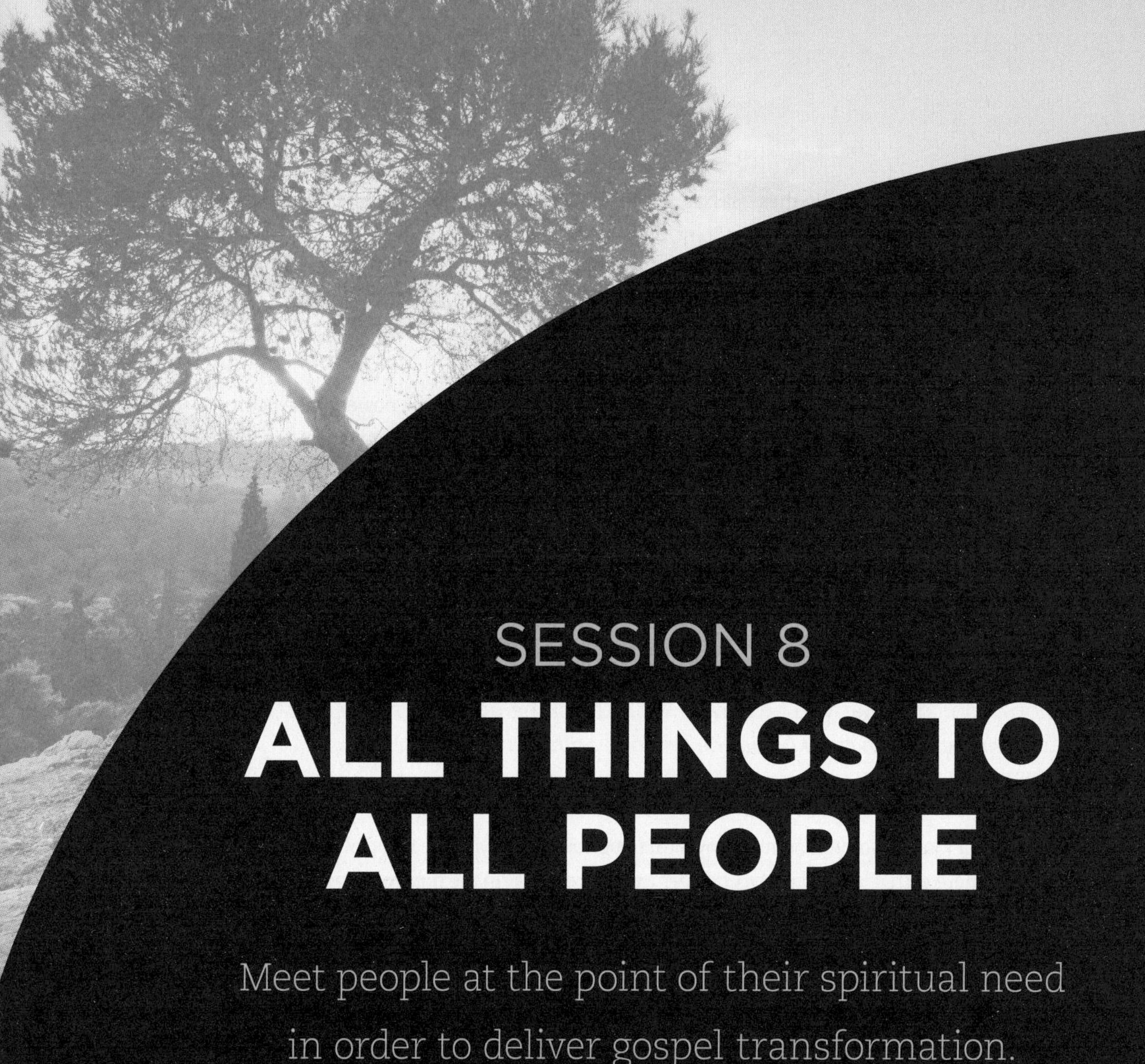

SESSION 8

ALL THINGS TO ALL PEOPLE

Meet people at the point of their spiritual need in order to deliver gospel transformation.

GET STARTED

REFLECT

In the previous session, we saw how believers can live by the power of the Holy Spirit. This isn't something that only happens on special occasions; rather, the Spirit can fill you and empower you every day of your life. This work of the Spirit should be an encouraging element in your spiritual journey. His presence and work in you will have a powerful impact on you and others.

In this session, we'll continue to explore God's mission for the world by exploring once again the truth that His gospel message is for all people—which means we must be adaptable in order to proclaim that gospel in all places.

Before we move forward, reflect back on what you learned and put into practice over the past week:

Which of the assignments did you explore this week? How did it go?

What did you learn or experience while reading the Bible?

What questions would you like to ask?

PRAY

Begin this session by connecting with God through prayer. Use the following guidelines as you speak with Him together:

- Pray that you would have a greater vision of God's work in the world and your place in it.
- Ask the Lord to continue to grow your passion to be a disciple who makes disciples.
- Pray that you would be passionate about seeing the Great Commission of Jesus come to completion.

INTRODUCTION

The world is filled with a vast array of people. Every day we see the differences among us—differences that are both slight and significant. These can be as simple as the distinction between someone from the Northern United States who likes unsweetened tea to a Southerner who only drinks sweet tea.

Of course, the differences can also be much greater.

We associate most often with people who are similar to us. That's natural. Hanging out with friends who have the same ethnic group, cultural upbringing, and life goals just makes friendships a bit easier. But when we begin to see and experience the differences between people, it can make for a much richer life.

Consider the city or region where you live. It likely has people from various parts of your state, country, and the world. As we know, any hint of prejudice doesn't make us look like Jesus. In fact, it carries us far away from a life like His. The Bible is explicit that favoritism in any form is strictly forbidden. Instead, as believers, we should be leading the way of living in such a way that all feel welcome in our lives.

Such a lifestyle isn't always natural for people. But it's usually attractive.

What do you like best about different cultures?

How have you personally benefited from exposure to different types of people?

When the Roman Empire ruled the Middle East and much of the surrounding lands, favoritism and social bias were commonplace. The church was filled with Christ followers who lived contrary to the social norm. They chose to invest, invite, and include those who looked or lived differently. All that mattered was a common commitment to have Christ as Lord.

In this session, we'll look more deeply at how the gospel is for all people. Recognizing its potential for touching every life will change how we approach disciple-making in our own communities.

KNOW THE STORY

Much of the Book of Acts records the travels and missionary work of the apostle Paul, who started as an enemy of the church but became a faithful disciple of Christ. One of those journeys took Paul to Athens, Greece. The heart Paul displayed for the people of that city should serve as a model for our mission in our culture.

16 While Paul was waiting for them in Athens, he was deeply
distressed when he saw that the city was full of idols. 17 So he
reasoned in the synagogue with the Jews and with those who
worshiped God, as well as in the marketplace every day with
those who happened to be there. 18 Some of the Epicurean and
Stoic philosophers also debated with him. Some said, "What is
this ignorant show-off trying to say?" Others replied, "He seems
to be a preacher of foreign deities"—because he was telling the
good news about Jesus and the resurrection.

19 They took him and brought him to the Areopagus, and said,
"May we learn about this new teaching you are presenting?
20 Because what you say sounds strange to us, and we want to
know what these things mean." 21 Now all the Athenians and
the foreigners residing there spent their time on nothing else
but telling or hearing something new.

22 Paul stood in the middle of the Areopagus and said: "People of
Athens! I see that you are extremely religious in every respect.
23 For as I was passing through and observing the objects of your
worship, I even found an altar on which was inscribed: 'To an
Unknown God.' Therefore, what you worship in ignorance, this I
proclaim to you."
ACTS 17:16-23

Where do you see similarities between the culture of Athens and our culture? Differences?

How would you describe Paul's attitude and posture?

UNPACK THE STORY

UNDERSTANDING REALITY

The world is what the world is. The church sometimes forgets that fact. As believers, we're tempted to hide from the world, shelter our kids, and hope we don't get stained by the problems the world presents. But the early church took a different approach.

When we look at the leaders and members of the early church, we see a community seeking to engage and transform the culture. That's what Paul was doing in Athens. He wanted to carry the gospel to people who were not like himself, and so he made it a priority to understand them.

In some ways, Paul relied on his pre-conversion life in order to know how to address the lost within a city like Athens. He didn't expect religious leaders from the Jewish temple to show up at the worship gathering of the Christian church. So, Paul sought them out on their own turf. He went to the temple to engage those who sought the one, true God. We should take note that Paul didn't go there to yell, pester, or harass his fellow Jews. He reasoned with them. Because Paul trusted in the truth of the gospel, he could present it with assurance and calmness.

Paul wanted to carry the gospel to people who were not like himself, and so he made it a priority to understand them.

Paul also went to the marketplace. Athens was an important city for commerce. It held a wide variety of people from across the Roman Empire who were intent on doing business. So he went to find them. To talk with them. To engage with them.

How would you summarize the primary goals of the people within today's culture? What are they looking for?

What are some specific elements that make your community and your culture unique?

Paul did all this because it grieved his heart to see a city filled with idols. Athens was characterized by large monuments, dedicated worship areas, small figures tucked away in corners, and even a hilltop with a huge temple dedicated to false gods. It troubled Paul's heart to see so many people headed into eternity without the hope he'd received through Jesus Christ.

SEEKING COMMITMENT

Paul never seemed to back down from adversity. In fact, he used any adversity he encountered as a tool for proclaiming the gospel. So, when Paul was ridiculed by different philosophers in the Athenian marketplace, he didn't run away. He didn't spew hatred in order to hurt them back. He humbly stood his ground—which is how he ended up with an invitation to share more about the gospel at the Areopagus.

Read Paul's message at the Areopagus in Acts 17:22-31. What do you like best about his message?

The Athenians were looking for a way to worship the powers of the universe. They wanted to please the entities that had power to create, sustain, make their crops fruitful, or ease the pain of a disease. They sacrificed to the gods they thought could bring victory in battle or increase their fertility. They went about their worship by making carvings from wood, stone, and all sorts of materials.

Paul addressed these falsehoods directly by telling the truth. Yet Paul wasn't looking for people to only listen politely to what he said. He wanted more:

> 30 "Therefore, having overlooked the times of ignorance, God now commands all people everywhere to repent, 31 because he has set a day when he is going to judge the world in righteousness by the man he has appointed. He has provided proof of this to everyone by raising him from the dead."
> ACTS 17:30-31

Paul's claim that Jesus had been raised from the dead demanded a response.

Paul's claim that Jesus had been raised from the dead demanded a response. It demanded repentance—turning away from sin and turning toward God. Paul wanted to engage the culture of Athens in order to produce good, so he called the people to commit.

How do you feel about calling others to repent? Why?

ENGAGE

We have the same responsibility as Paul. You probably don't live in Athens, and you may not walk among a valley of idols and graven images—but you know that a majority of people in your community are living far away from a true understanding of Jesus. Therefore, your task is to determine how much they do know and how open they are to hearing the gospel.

As part of that task, commit to taking a prayer walk around your community. Join with the members of your group to walk through the streets in your neighborhoods and pray for the people there. Use the following questions to plan out your walk as a group:

When will we walk and pray together?

Where will we walk and pray, specifically?

What specific requests will we bring to God as we walk and pray?

PRAYER REQUESTS

WEEKLY ACTIVITIES

In addition to studying God's Word, work with your group leader to create a plan for personal study, worship, and application between now and the next session. Select from the following optional activities to match your personal preferences and available time.

Worship

- [x] Read your Bible. Complete the reading plan on page 112.
- [ ] Spend time with God by engaging the devotional experience on page 113.

Personal Study

- [ ] Read and interact with "Connecting with Everyone" on page 114.
- [ ] Read and interact with "Serving with Purpose" on page 116.

Application

- [ ] Memorize Acts 17:30-31: "Therefore, having overlooked the times of ignorance, God now commands all people everywhere to repent, because he has set a day when he is going to judge the world in righteousness by the man he has appointed. He has provided proof of this to everyone by raising him from the dead."
- [ ] In the same way that your group will do a prayer walk around a portion of your community, commit to walking the streets of your specific neighborhood and praying for the people who live and work close to you. Pray for ways to engage those people with the gospel.
- [ ] Seek a better understanding of the gospel in order to better proclaim the gospel to others. Read a book, listen to a sermon, download a podcast—choose to increase what you know about God's Word and His gospel.
- [ ] Continue journaling throughout the week. Pay special attention to moments when you're able to connect with someone in a new or meaningful way.
- [ ] Other:

READING PLAN

Read through the following Scripture passages this week. Use the space provided to record your thoughts and responses.

Day 1
Acts 16:10-15

Day 2
1 Corinthians 9:19-23

Day 3
Acts 16:11-15

Day 4
Acts 14:8-20

Day 5
Acts 18:24-28

Day 6
Romans 10:14-17

Day 7
Acts 26:1-11

HEALTHY GROUPS, HEALTHY GOALS

Sharing our faith is something that needs encouragement. As a discipline, evangelism is also helped along by accountability. Thankfully, being part of a healthy group or mentoring relationship can help you accomplish both of those goals.

The author of Hebrews made a plea for both encouragement and accountability in the early church:

> 12 Watch out, brothers and sisters, so that there won't be in any of you an evil,
> unbelieving heart that turns away from the living God. 13 But encourage each
> other daily, while it is still called today, so that none of you is hardened by sin's
> deception. 14 For we have become participants in Christ if we hold firmly until
> the end the reality that we had at the start.
> HEBREWS 3:12-14

This is an unbelievably practical command for anyone who seeks to live as a disciple of Jesus. Is today still called today? Then I should watch out for the influence of sin in my life and in the lives of those I care about. Is today still called today? Then I should choose to encourage those who are following Christ with me and around me, so that each of our hearts can remain soft to the gospel.

And I should do each of these things before "today" becomes "tomorrow."

How have you benefited from sharing accountability with other Christians?

How have you benefited from being encouraged by other Christians?

How have you benefited from choosing to encourage others?

What obstacles may be preventing you from more actively sharing accountability and encouragement with those closest to you?

PERSONAL STUDY

CONNECTING WITH EVERYONE

The work of being a disciple and a disciple-maker means helping everyone find what you have found, receive what you have received, and live like you are trying to live within God's kingdom. There's just one problem: not everyone is like you. There are cultural barriers, ethnic differences, and lots of other factors that get in the way of our ability to form relationships—and forming relationships is a key part of sharing the gospel.

Still, as believers, we know that everyone shares a common need for salvation. And that's a critical way to connect with others.

When Paul walked through the streets of Athens, he saw that need. He felt that drive to connect with people that served him so well throughout his ministry. This drive didn't control him, but it was a guiding principle that made him a great ambassador for Christ.

Look at what Paul wrote to the Christians in the city of Corinth, which was a neighbor to Athens:

> 19 Although I am free from all and not anyone's slave, I have made myself
> a slave to everyone, in order to win more people. 20 To the Jews I became
> like a Jew, to win Jews; to those under the law, like one under the law—
> though I myself am not under the law—to win those under the law. 21 To
> those who are without the law, like one without the law—though I am
> not without God's law but under the law of Christ—to win those without
> the law. 22 To the weak I became weak, in order to win the weak. I have
> become all things to all people, so that I may by every possible means
> save some. 23 Now I do all this because of the gospel, so that I may share in
> the blessings.
> 1 CORINTHIANS 9:19-23

What questions come to mind when you read these verses?

How would you summarize Paul's primary point or argument in these verses?

What principles from these verses can you apply in your efforts to serve Jesus and make disciples?

Paul never allowed anything but the gospel to serve as the source of his identity. He often used the phrase "in Christ" in his letters to the church. Because he was "in Christ," Paul knew he could be a servant to everyone—just as Christ gave Himself as a sacrifice in order to serve everyone by making a way for all people to receive salvation.

As we see from his words to the Corinthians, Paul knew that his identity in Christ actually freed him to serve people in even better ways. He was able to empathize with people's lives so that he could carry the gospel message to them. He sought to understand and engage slaves, Jews, Gentiles, and the weak—all so that he could be more effective in sharing the gospel with any who needed to hear it.

Of course, Paul didn't completely imitate these groups. He didn't let go of his faith in Christ when he "became like a Jew," for example. Paul maintained his identity as "in Christ" in all respects, even as he chose to become like others in some respects in order to reach them with the gospel.

We are called to do the same.

How would you rate your ability to empathize with or understand others?

1	2	3	4	5	6	7	8	9	10
Poor									Great

What are some dangers of seeking to become like other people in order to better engage them?

What steps can you take to imitate Paul's strategy of becoming like others in order to share the gospel?

PERSONAL STUDY 2

SERVING WITH PURPOSE

Paul always had a purpose in mind when he took part in the work of disciple-making. He wanted Christ to be exalted, and he wanted to participate in God's grace being poured out to others. That's why he wrote, "Now I do all this because of the gospel, so that I may share in the blessings" (1 Cor. 9:23).

That raises an important question: what gets you up and going in the morning? What drives you to do the things you do? What motivations have made you the person you are?

How would you describe the primary goals you've been seeking to achieve today?

How would you summarize your primary goals and motivations for life in general?

What are your biggest dreams for your future?

Let's be frank: many people are living in a kind of survival mode these days. They're working jobs they barely like in order to pay bills and maintain a house that keeps them frustrated in order to keep a roof over the heads of people they feel are at least a little bit ungrateful. That may sound extreme, but it gets the point across.

Lots of people are just trying to get by. Lots of people are doing their best simply to muddle through each day. Including lots of Christians.

To what degree have you been living in the kind of "survival mode" described above?

1 2 3 4 5 6 7 8 9 10

Living in "survival mode" ... **Living with purpose**

To what degree are your friends and/or family members living in that kind of "survival mode"?

1 2 3 4 5 6 7 8 9 10

Living in "survival mode" **Living with purpose**

When you commit to being a disciple-maker, you do so because you've decided that the gospel is enough. It's enough to change your life, and it's enough to change the lives of others. On top of that, the gospel is completely enough to bring about a joyful journey of serving Jesus.

Back in 1 Corinthians 9, Paul also wrote that he wanted to "share in the blessings" of the gospel. Think about that for a moment.

When you do whatever it takes to be all things to all people so that some might be saved, you're a partner with God in His work. When you partner with Him, your life is enriched. You automatically get to know His grace and power on deeper levels. Your joy is magnified and your life has greater purpose. Talk about blessings!

In what ways has your purpose changed throughout your journey of following Jesus?

What are some additional areas in which you desire to partner with God and the work He is doing?

Let's conclude with another powerful thought from Paul's message to the Corinthians:

> Don't you know that the runners in a stadium all race, but only one receives the prize? Run in such a way to win the prize.
> 1 CORINTHIANS 9:24

It's in partnering with God to do whatever it takes to reach the lost with the gospel that a Christian can truly walk in the way of Christ. May that be your vision this week, and may that serve as your purpose in the weeks to come.

SESSION 9

PRODUCING SPIRITUAL FRUIT

We bear spiritual fruit only when we are walking closely with Jesus.

GET STARTED

REFLECT

We saw in the previous session that it's important for us to understand the culture in which we're making disciples. It's also necessary for us to be aware of the individual situations and personalities of those we're striving to move toward greater Christlikeness. If we don't remember that Jesus is the power behind disciple-making, however, we're not likely to achieve any of those goals.

As you prepare to explore the importance of producing spiritual fruit and the importance of Jesus being the power through which that happens, take a few minutes to reflect on your experiences over the past week:

Which of the assignments did you explore this week? How did it go?

What did you learn or experience while reading the Bible?

What questions would you like to ask?

PRAY

Begin this session by connecting with God through prayer. Use the following guidelines as you speak with Him together:

- Express your gratitude to God for the transformation you've seen in your own life throughout your journey of following Jesus.
- Thank God for giving us a model for disciple-making: Jesus Christ.
- Ask God for wisdom as you engage the Bible and learn what it means to "bear fruit."

INTRODUCTION

Most people feel they have a pretty good understanding of what a "fruit" is. We think of apples, bananas, lemons, and so on. Most people also feel they have a pretty good example of what a "vegetable" would be. We think of lettuce, spinach, broccoli, and more.

But what about tomatoes? Are they fruits or vegetables? Believe it or not, that question has sparked a lot of debate in recent centuries, both from the scientific community and the business world.

In the field of botany, for example, tomatoes are technically defined as fruit. That's because tomatoes contain seeds and are developed from the ovary of a flowering plant, which is the scientific definition of a fruit. Vegetables, on the other hand, are the edible parts of plants that come from everything other than the ovary—roots, stalks, leaves, and so on.

In the business world, however, tomatoes are traditionally categorized as vegetables. In fact, the Supreme Court itself established this categorization in 1893 after a long legal battle between John Nix, the owner of a large produce company, and the State of New York. In those days, New York imposed a large import tax on vegetables, but not fruits. And since John Nix knew that tomatoes were scientifically classified as fruits, he declined to pay the tax on all of his imported tomatoes. The Supreme Court ruled against him, however, stating that tomatoes were primarily sold and used as vegetables, rather than fruits.

What fruits would you have the hardest time living without?

What have you been taught about the concept of "spiritual fruit" in the Christian life?

While there's a surprising amount of debate regarding the "fruitiness" of tomatoes, there's no debate about the critical importance of spiritual fruit in the Christian life. As we'll see in this session, disciples of Jesus are commanded throughout Scripture to produce spiritual fruit, both in themselves and others.

And as we'll also see, we have no ability to produce that fruit on our own.

KNOW THE STORY

When wise disciple-makers are about to leave their disciples on their own, they spend their last hours giving those disciples essential information that will aid them in accomplishing their goals and purposes in the future.

Jesus is a wise disciple-maker. And we can find some of His final words to His disciples in what is known as the "Farewell Discourse" in the Book of John. What you're about to read is part of Jesus' heartfelt words to the apostles—some of His final directions for His disciples. These words teach us that remaining connected to Jesus, even in His visible absence, was vital to His first disciples then, and is essential to His disciples today.

> 1 "I am the true vine, and my Father is the gardener. 2 Every
> branch in me that does not produce fruit he removes, and he
> prunes every branch that produces fruit so that it will produce
> more fruit. 3 You are already clean because of the word I have
> spoken to you. 4 Remain in me, and I in you. Just as a branch is
> unable to produce fruit by itself unless it remains on the vine,
> neither can you unless you remain in me. 5 I am the vine; you
> are the branches. The one who remains in me and I in him
> produces much fruit, because you can do nothing without me.
> 6 If anyone does not remain in me, he is thrown aside like a
> branch and he withers. They gather them, throw them into the
> fire, and they are burned. 7 If you remain in me and my words
> remain in you, ask whatever you want and it will be done for
> you. 8 My Father is glorified by this: that you produce much fruit
> and prove to be my disciples."
> JOHN 15:1-8

What are the key images in these verses, and what do those images communicate?

How would you describe what it means to "produce fruit" as a disciple of Jesus?

UNPACK THE STORY

DISCIPLES PRODUCE FRUIT

According to John 15, there are two types of people who claim to follow Jesus: those who don't produce spiritual fruit and those who do. This "fruit" that Jesus expects from His followers starts with developing a personal character that mirrors Jesus' character. It also includes the gathering of new believers into His kingdom—the practice of sharing the gospel message and making new disciples.

The people in the first group, those who are not bearing fruit, are confused about their connection to Christ. They are cultural Christians—they may go to church, they may know the right things to say, they may know the right things to do, and they may firmly believe they are genuine believers. But they're wrong, because they have produced no fruit. They are spiritually dead.

This is vitally important information, because verse 6 of Jesus' discourse makes it clear that unfruitful branches will be removed from the vine. They will be gathered together, thrown into the fire, and burned. This is a picture of judgment.

When we live as Jesus' disciples in this world, we will produce fruit for His kingdom.

What are some factors that cause people to believe they are following Jesus when they are not?

Who do you know who consistently produces spiritual fruit for God's kingdom?

The second category of people Jesus speaks of in this analogy is branches that do bear fruit. These are people who have a right and healthy relationship with Christ. They are truly His disciples.

Yet notice the emphasis in the second half of verse 2: "he prunes every branch that produces fruit so that it will produce more fruit." When we live as Jesus' disciples in this world, we will produce fruit for His kingdom. And when we produce fruit, we will be pruned by God Himself.

This idea of being pruned means that God will remove interests and activities that get in the way of bearing spiritual fruit. It's God's desire for His followers to bear more and more fruit, not to be content with our past evangelistic accomplishments.

DISCIPLE-MAKERS STAY CONNECTED TO JESUS

In order to be effective disciple-makers, Jesus said we must "remain" in Him. In fact, He made it clear that we can accomplish absolutely nothing of worth unless we remain in Him (see v. 5). This concept makes sense to us because of Jesus' effective use of imagery. We've all seen branches lying on the ground, and we understand perfectly well that those branches cannot produce anything on their own.

The Greek word translated as "remain" in John 15 is *meno*. It means "to stay, stand fast, stay where you are, not stir, or to remain as before." By emphasizing this word, Jesus wanted His disciples to realize their dependence on Him and their need to stay in continual, unceasing fellowship with Him.

He wants the same for us. Without this ongoing connection, no real fruit will come from our ministries or our efforts to share the gospel.

When have you been especially aware of (or blessed by) your connection to Jesus?

What are practical ways to maintain your awareness of that connection throughout each day?

One result of remaining in Christ as His disciples is that we will see great power in our prayers. Jesus made a powerful promise in verse 7: "If you remain in me and my words remain in you, ask whatever you want and it will be done for you." When we maintain a constant communion with God through prayer, we should develop a holy confidence as we pray.

Of course, this doesn't mean God is a genie in a bottle who gives us whatever we want. When we're in a more constant communion with Jesus, and when we know His Word, our prayers will be more aligned with His will—they will bring glory to Him.

Jesus wanted His disciples to realize their dependence on Him and their need to stay in continual, unceasing fellowship with Him.

How would you like to see your prayer life improve?

ENGAGE

Understanding that you must rely on Jesus if you're going to bear spiritual fruit may demand a significant change in both your thinking and your daily lifestyle. Use the space below to record your routine on a typical day. Then write out some changes you could make to more fully "remain" in Christ.

My daily routine for the past month:	**Changes I can make to "remain" in Christ:**
Early Morning	
Morning	
Afternoon	
Evening	

What is one key change you want to make to your daily routine starting tomorrow?

Who can help you make that change and maintain it going forward?

PRAYER REQUESTS

In addition to studying God's Word, work with your group leader to create a plan for personal study, worship, and application between now and the next session. Select from the following optional activities to match your personal preferences and available time.

Worship

- [x] Read your Bible. Complete the reading plan on page 126.

- [ ] Spend time with God by engaging the devotional experience on page 127.

Personal Study

- [ ] Read and interact with "How to Produce Fruit" on page 128.

- [ ] Read and interact with "How to Stay Connected to the Vine" on page 130.

Application

- [ ] Memorize John 15:5: "I am the vine; you are the branches. The one who remains in me and I in him produces much fruit, because you can do nothing without me."

- [ ] You will be much more consistent spending time with God in prayer and Bible study on a daily basis if you calendar that time each. Take your calendar and schedule 30-60 minutes for spending time with God at least 5 days a week. Make it official.

- [ ] Submit to God's desire for you to produce spiritual fruit by meeting with someone this week who needs to start a relationship with Jesus. Tell them your story, how you became a follower of Jesus, and how He has affected your life.

- [ ] Continue journaling, writing down what God says to you as you spend time in prayer and in studying His Word.

- [ ] Other:

WORSHIP

READING PLAN

Read through the following Scripture passages this week. Use the space provided to record your thoughts and responses.

Day 1
Acts 3:1-17

Day 2
Luke 13:6-9

Day 3
John 15:1-16

Day 4
Colossians 1:1-6

Day 5
Psalm 62:1-12

Day 6
2 Corinthians 12:1-10

Day 7
Philippians 4:10-20

LETTING GO

Many Christians striving to live as disciple-makers find themselves struggling with being dependent on God. After all, we're part of a culture that declares to us again and again that whatever we accomplish depends on us—and us alone. When we graduate from high school or college, we hear speeches challenging us to accomplish great things and reminding us that, "You can accomplish anything you set your mind to."

We're inundated with messages from movies and other stories claiming that we determine our life agenda, and that we can make our goals become a reality if we work hard enough, go against the grain, and refuse to settle for the kind of life the authorities want to squeeze us into.

Here's the truth: we cannot be effective disciple-makers if we embrace this mindset of self-actualization from our culture. Instead, we must embrace the truth that we are dependent on Jesus—just as Jesus was dependent on the Father during His time on earth. We must be in constant contact with God if we want our lives to matter for eternity.

Consider these passages, and read them slowly:

> Very early in the morning, while it was still dark, [Jesus] got up, went out, and made his way to a deserted place; and there he was praying.
> MARK 1:35

> After dismissing the crowds, [Jesus] went up on the mountain by himself to pray. Well into the night, he was there alone.
> MATTHEW 14:23

> Therefore, when Jesus realized that they were about to come and take him by force to make him king, he withdrew again to the mountain by himself.
> JOHN 6:15

What steps did Jesus take in order to spend time with the Father?

What are steps you need to take in order spend time alone with God?

HOW TO PRODUCE FRUIT

Bearing fruit demands that disciples of Jesus be proactive in seeking out those who are in need of salvation. Jesus is the perfect example of Someone who produced spiritual fruit throughout His life on earth. Therefore, we can learn more about how to produce fruit ourselves by examining His choices and focusing on the kinds of people to whom He took the gospel. Specifically, following Jesus' example will help us open our hearts and lives to people we might otherwise overlook.

We know from Scripture that Jesus, our example, came to "seek and to save the lost" (Luke 19:10). We also know that these "lost" individuals were often the kind of people that the religious types of Jesus day were more likely to judge than help.

For example, Jesus was known throughout His community for bringing the gospel to "tax collectors and sinners" (Luke 5:30). That is, Jesus specifically connected with people who had committed fraud by stealing from the Jewish community—people who'd been ostracized by the religious elites. In fact, Jesus was so welcoming to these unwelcomed people that Luke 15:1 tells us of an instance when, "All the tax collectors and sinners were approaching to listen to him."

All of them!

What categories of people are often ostracized or excluded in our culture today?

What categories of people are often ostracized or excluded in your community, specifically?

Zacchaeus was a chief tax collector in the region where Jesus lived and ministered. That meant Zacchaeus had oversight of many other tax collectors in that region. He was known as a servant of the Romans and a traitor to his people.

What people didn't know, however, was that Zacchaeus was in pursuit of a life that had meaning. He wanted something more than he'd achieved through his money and his power—the kind of life he could only find if he sought out and embraced the gospel of Jesus Christ.

Of course, Jesus knew what Zacchaeus was seeking. And Jesus saw an opportunity to produce fruit:

> 1 [Jesus] entered Jericho and was passing through. 2 There was a man
> named Zacchaeus who was a chief tax collector, and he was rich. 3 He was
> trying to see who Jesus was, but he was not able because of the crowd,
> since he was a short man. 4 So running ahead, he climbed up a sycamore
> tree to see Jesus, since he was about to pass that way. 5 When Jesus came
> to the place, he looked up and said to him, "Zacchaeus, hurry and come
> down because today it is necessary for me to stay at your house."
>
> 6 So he quickly came down and welcomed him joyfully. 7 All who saw it
> began to complain, "He's gone to stay with a sinful man."
>
> 8 But Zacchaeus stood there and said to the Lord, "Look, I'll give half of
> my possessions to the poor, Lord. And if I have extorted anything from
> anyone, I'll pay back four times as much."
>
> 9 "Today salvation has come to this house," Jesus told him, "because he too
> is a son of Abraham. 10 For the Son of Man has come to seek and to save
> the lost."
>
> LUKE 19:1-10

How would you describe Jesus' attitude toward Zacchaeus?

What do Zacchaeus's actions reveal about the possible mindset of those who don't know Jesus?

When we take the gospel to those who've been pushed aside or judged as evil by society, we produce spiritual fruit. We also provide opportunities for others to watch our actions and see the power of ministering to those on the fringes. As you seek to follow Jesus' example, choose to be a model not only on how to verbalize the gospel message to others, but also how to relate, in love, with those who are practicing sinful behaviors—with those in need of a Savior.

PERSONAL STUDY 2

HOW TO STAY CONNECTED TO THE VINE

As we've seen, Jesus is the Source for anything and everything we accomplish as His disciples. When we walk with Him each day, we will experience His power and we will see Him work through us in amazing ways.

The early church is a prime example of this principle. Acts 2 tells us that those early believers "devoted themselves to the apostles' teaching, to the fellowship, to the breaking of bread, and to prayer" (v. 42). As a result, they consistently saw God work in miraculous ways.

Peter was a leader in the early church and one of those believers. Therefore, it shouldn't be a surprise to see what God accomplished through his life and ministry. For example:

> 32 As Peter was traveling from place to place, he also came down to the
> saints who lived in Lydda. 33 There he found a man named Aeneas, who
> was paralyzed and had been bedridden for eight years. 34 Peter said to
> him, "Aeneas, Jesus Christ heals you. Get up and make your bed," and
> immediately he got up. 35 So all who lived in Lydda and Sharon saw him
> and turned to the Lord.
> ACTS 9:32-35

What stands out about Peter's words to Aeneas?

What were the short-term and long-term effects of the miracle that God worked through Peter?

Notice how Peter addressed the paralyzed man: "Aeneas, Jesus Christ heals you." Peter could have taken the credit for this miracle. At the least, he could have tried sharing the glory along with Jesus. That kind of temptation is a natural part of human nature.

But Peter knew better. He knew that any power demonstrated in his life came through one and only Source—Jesus Christ, the Vine. Peter also understood that seeking to glorify ourselves is one of the quickest ways for us to become disconnected from God's power.

So then, what are some keys to remaining connected to Jesus, the Vine, and experiencing His power? Peter gave the following advice in one of his letters to the early church:

> 1 Therefore, rid yourselves of all malice, all deceit, hypocrisy, envy, and
> all slander. 2 Like newborn infants, desire the pure milk of the word, so
> that you may grow up into your salvation, 3 if you have tasted that the
> Lord is good. 4 As you come to him, a living stone—rejected by people but
> chosen and honored by God— 5 you yourselves, as living stones, a spiritual
> house, are being built to be a holy priesthood to offer spiritual sacrifices
> acceptable to God through Jesus Christ.
> 1 PETER 2:1-5

What are some of the key images contained in these verses?

What do those images communicate?

What specific practices does Peter recommend for maintaining our connection with Jesus?

Which of these practices would make a significant impact in your life?

In many ways, staying connected with Jesus is like eating a healthy diet. Most of us know almost instinctively which foods are healthy and which are not. It's simply a matter of doing what we know we should do.

In the same way, if we're going to influence the world for Christ, then every one of Christ's disciples must walk with Him, accomplish His work, give Him the credit, verbalize through whom the work was accomplished, and allow the name of Jesus to transform those He chooses.

SESSION 10

A COMMITMENT TO DISCIPLESHIP

Learn from the examples of effective disciple-makers in God's Word

GET STARTED

REFLECT

In the last session, we saw our need for the power of Christ working through us in order to produce fruit for God's kingdom. Remaining in Christ demands that we journey with Him on an ongoing, daily, all-the-time basis. This principle is foundational to transformational disciple-making.

During this session, we're going to explore Paul's example in discipling a young pastor named Timothy. Before we dive into the Scripture, however, take a few minutes to discuss your experiences in recent days.

Which of the assignments did you explore this week? How did it go?

What did you learn or experience while reading the Bible?

What questions would you like to ask?

PRAY

Begin this session by connecting with God through prayer. Use the following guidelines as you speak with Him together:

- Express your gratitude to God for the process of discipleship, which allows you to both bless and be blessed as you follow Christ.
- Thank God for giving us the book of Timothy, through which we can read the specific words of a disciple-maker to the one he discipled.
- Ask God for wisdom as you engage the Bible and learn more and more about what it means to be a disciple-maker.

INTRODUCTION

Passing the baton is a relatively simple act in the world of track-and-field relay races. One runner races around the track, then ends his or her turn by handing the 12-inch long cylindrical stick to the next runner, who then continues the race. Successful passes are a necessary element for any team hoping to stand on the podium with medals in hand.

Of course, things don't always go as planned.

In the 2008 Olympic Games, both the U.S. men's and women's 4 x 100 meter relay teams were eliminated in the first round of competition because of baton drops. These failures were especially devastating because the United States track team has a sterling history in that event. Since 1932, American women's teams have won 11 gold medals in the 100-meter relay. That's equal to the gold count from all other countries combined. Since 1920, the American men's relay team has won gold at 15 of the 21 Olympic games. In short, America has dominated that event for a century.

But not in 2008. One moment in time, one second of miscalculation, one oversight, left the runners full of defeat rather than full of pride.

What's one of your favorite Olympic events? Why?

What's something you've learned in your time as a disciple of Jesus that you're excited to pass along to the next generation of disciples?

Purposefully and wisely passing the baton is a key skill in relay races—but it's even more essential in disciple-making.

If even one generation of disciple-makers were to shun the responsibility for discipleship or use non-biblical practices to make disciples, the consequences would be disastrous. Not only would that generation lose the race to accomplish God's purposes, but the next generation of believers would lack the essential principles and practices to continue passing that baton forward into the future.

KNOW THE STORY

While visiting Asia Minor, the apostle Paul invited a young disciple named Timothy to join his second missionary journey (see Acts 16:1-5). That encounter began a discipleship relationship between the two men that lasted for several years. Thankfully, we have the privilege of seeing "behind the curtain" of that relationship because of the letters Paul wrote to encourage and support Timothy, whom he called "my true son in the faith" (1 Tim. 1:2).

> 3 I thank God, whom I serve with a clear conscience as my
> ancestors did, when I constantly remember you in my prayers
> night and day. 4 Remembering your tears, I long to see you so
> that I may be filled with joy. 5 I recall your sincere faith that first
> lived in your grandmother Lois and in your mother Eunice and
> now, I am convinced, is in you also.
>
> 6 Therefore, I remind you to rekindle the gift of God that is in
> you through the laying on of my hands. 7 For God has not given
> us a spirit of fear, but one of power, love, and sound judgment.
> 2 TIMOTHY 1:3-7

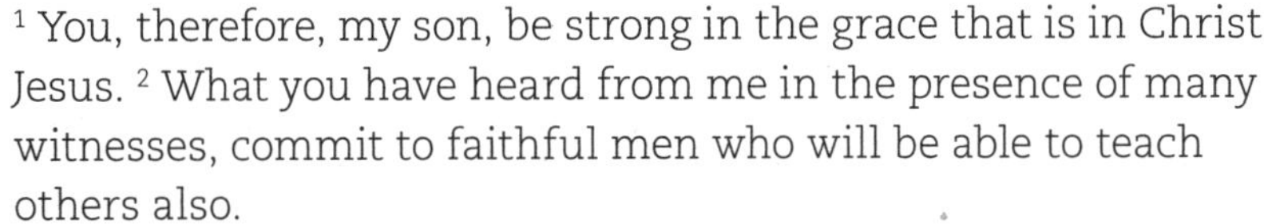

> 1 You, therefore, my son, be strong in the grace that is in Christ
> Jesus. 2 What you have heard from me in the presence of many
> witnesses, commit to faithful men who will be able to teach
> others also.
>
> 3 Share in suffering as a good soldier of Christ Jesus. 4 No one
> serving as a soldier gets entangled in the concerns of civilian
> life; he seeks to please the commanding officer. 5 Also, if anyone
> competes as an athlete, he is not crowned unless he competes
> according to the rules. 6 The hardworking farmer ought to be
> the first to get a share of the crops. 7 Consider what I say, for the
> Lord will give you understanding in everything.
> 2 TIMOTHY 2:1-7

How many generations of disciples are present in these verses?

How do these verses illustrate the process of discipleship?

UNPACK THE STORY

DISCIPLE-MAKERS SHOW LOVE

There are many Christians today—and even many disciple-makers—who share a common misunderstanding about the nature of discipleship. Specifically, many people feel that making disciples is mostly an intellectual process. In this view, one person engages to teach another person what to believe, how to behave, and what mistakes should be avoided. This kind of discipleship is all about the transfer of information.

When we look at biblical examples of disciple-making, however, we find a different story. Jesus, for example, cared deeply for His disciples. He lived with them day in and day out, He showed incredible patience with their repeated failures, and He called them His friends. (See John 15:15.)

Similarly, Paul's connection with Timothy was deeply personal and filled with mutual love.

Read once again through 2 Timothy 1:3-7; 2:1-7. Where do you see evidence of an emotional connection?

What are some of the ways you've been blessed through key relationships in your life?

Paul mentioned praying for Timothy on several occasions, and we must do the same for those who join us in the process of discipleship.

There's one ingredient that's necessary for the development of any type of relationship: time. Just as children need a significant amount of time with their parents in order to develop and growth in a healthy way, spiritual children need time with their spiritual parents in order to become fully mature as disciples of Christ. In fact, these were among Paul's last words at the end of his second epistle to Timothy: "Make every effort to come to me soon" (2 Tim. 4:9).

Another key ingredient is prayer. Paul mentioned praying for Timothy on several occasions, and we must do the same for those who join us in the process of discipleship.

How will you set aside time for discipleship in your daily routine? For prayer?

DISCIPLE-MAKERS SHOW THE WAY

You may have heard someone make the following statement about their children: "I'm not supposed to be their friend; I'm supposed to be their parent." This is one of the complicated principles that's both true and not true. On the one hand, it's certainly possible for good parents to be friends with their children—to spend time with them and enjoy their company. On the other hand, it's not possible for good parents to be *only* friends to their children, or *primarily* friends; the relationship must go deeper to be productive.

The same is true for the relationship between disciple-makers and their disciples. It's important for these relationships to begin with friendship, but they must not end there. Disciple-makers have an active role in helping others grow and develop and mature as disciples of Jesus.

That's what we see in the relationship between Paul and Timothy.

Read once again through 2 Timothy 1:3-7; 2:1-7. Where do you see Paul guiding Timothy—even correcting him?

What are your expectations for your current relationships that involve discipleship?

Disciple-makers are not spiritual accountants.

Disciple-makers should view themselves as spiritual parents, which includes the responsibility of both supporting and guiding those under their spiritual care. Disciples should view themselves as spiritual children, which means demonstrating a genuine respect for those above them—and making a genuine effort to grow.

At the same time, the entire discipleship relationship will be most beneficial for everyone involved when it's grounded in the mutual love explored on the previous page.

Disciple-makers are not spiritual accountants. We don't dig through the details of people's lives, ready to pounce once any error is discovered and demand it be corrected. There will certainly be times where correction is needed. There will even be moments of disappointment or regret. Yet we as disciple-makers should always be guided by our knowledge of how far we've come in our own journeys toward Christ—and how far we still have to go.

ENGAGE

Disciple-makers must sometimes remind disciples about the expectations and practices connected with following Christ. Here are some of the reminders Paul offered Timothy during his epistles. Use these assessments to evaluate yourself, or to help those you are discipling evaluate themselves.

"Rekindle the gift of God"—don't be sluggish in your faith.

1 2 3 4 5 6 7 8 9 10

Not doing well **Doing well**

"God has not given us a spirit of fear, but one of power, love, and sound judgment"—be bold as you follow Christ.

1 2 3 4 5 6 7 8 9 10

Not doing well **Doing well**

"What you have heard from me ... commit to faithful men who will be able to teach others also"—be active in discipling others.

1 2 3 4 5 6 7 8 9 10

Not doing well **Doing well**

"Share in suffering as a good soldier of Christ Jesus"—be willing to sacrifice your own comforts and desires.

1 2 3 4 5 6 7 8 9 10

Not doing well **Doing well**

PRAYER REQUESTS

....

....

....

WEEKLY ACTIVITIES

In addition to studying God's Word, work with your group leader to create a plan for personal study, worship, and application between now and the next session. Select from the following optional activities to match your personal preferences and available time.

Worship

- [x] Read your Bible. Complete the reading plan on page 140.
- [ ] Spend time with God by engaging the devotional experience on page 141.

Personal Study

- [ ] Read and interact with "Spiritual Stages of Growth" on page 142.
- [ ] Read and interact with "Spiritual Guidance" on page 144.

Application

- [ ] Memorize 2 Timothy 2:2: "What you have heard from me in the presence of many witnesses, commit to faithful men who will be able to teach others also."
- [ ] Write down the name of a mature disciple you know and respect. Make a list of the characteristics you see in them that mirror the attitudes and actions of Jesus. Meet with them to learn how they are growing toward Christ-likeness.
- [ ] Begin making a list of people you may want to disciple. Pray over this list each day, asking God to direct you to the right person and give you opportunities to assess their current level of spiritual maturity.
- [ ] Take some time to evaluate your current experiences with the discipleship process. What's going well? What needs work? Who can you talk with to find ideas for making your own discipleship and your efforts at disciple-making more productive?
- [ ] Other:

WORSHIP

READING PLAN

Read through the following Scripture passages this week. Use the space provided to record your thoughts and responses.

Day 1
Matthew 28:1-20

Day 2
Colossians 1:1-29

Day 3
John 6:60-71

Day 4
Acts 17:1-15

Day 5
John 17:1-26

Day 6
1 Peter 4:7-19

Day 7
1 Kings 19:19-21

BEING TIMOTHY

Many followers of Jesus are capable of seeing themselves as disciples, but that's where their image of their role in the disciple-making flow chart ends. They know they have a responsibility to grow spiritually, and they focus only on that process. They see themselves as disciples, but not disciple-makers.

However, in order for us to accomplish the goals Jesus gave us—and in order for us to grow to full maturity—we need to be both disciples and disciple-makers. We are called to be learning from others while at the same time teaching others. Both are key elements in following Jesus.

We see this most vividly in Timothy. Because as Paul was discipling Timothy, Timothy was discipling others:

> What you have heard from me in the presence of many witnesses, commit to faithful men who will be able to teach others also.
> 2 TIMOTHY 2:2

Notice the four generations of disciples revealed in this convicting passage.

- Generation 1: Paul
- Generation 2: Timothy
- Generation 3: Faithful men
- Generation 4: Others

What are some obstacles that keep people from striving to become disciple-makers?

How would you describe your past experiences with disciple-making?

How would you describe your future goals as a disciple-maker?

PERSONAL STUDY

SPIRITUAL STAGES OF GROWTH

Every Christ-follower is a disciple, but not every disciple is at the exact same stage of spiritual growth. There are many levels of growth in Christ. The apostle John pointed out some of these levels in one of his epistles to the early church:

> 12 I am writing to you, little children,
> since your sins have been forgiven
> on account of his name.
> 13 I am writing to you, fathers,
> because you have come to know
> the one who is from the beginning.
> I am writing to you, young men,
> because you have conquered the evil one.
> 14 I have written to you, children,
> because you have come to know the Father.
> I have written to you, fathers,
> because you have come to know
> the one who is from the beginning.
> I have written to you, young men,
> because you are strong,
> God's word remains in you,
> and you have conquered the evil one.
> 1 JOHN 2:12-14

What are some of the spiritual stages mentioned in these verses?

How would you describe your current stage of spiritual growth?

How long would you say you've been working through this stage?

How would you summarize your hopes for spiritual growth in the future?

It's also important to point out that, just as different people can be at different stages of spiritual growth, those we disciple will also move through those stages at different speeds. When we look at Paul's efforts at discipleship, for example, it's clear that Timothy moved relatively quickly through his early stages of spiritual growth:

> 1 Paul went on to Derbe and Lystra, where there was a disciple named
> Timothy, the son of a believing Jewish woman, but his father was a Greek.
> 2 The brothers and sisters at Lystra and Iconium spoke highly of him.
> 3 Paul wanted Timothy to go with him; so he took him and circumcised
> him because of the Jews who were in those places, since they all knew
> that his father was a Greek. 4 As they traveled through the towns, they
> delivered the decisions reached by the apostles and elders at Jerusalem
> for the people to observe. 5 So the churches were strengthened in the faith
> and grew daily in numbers.
> ACTS 16:1-5

This is a rapid process. Paul met Timothy, and they evidently clicked. Timothy was already established as a Christian, but Paul invested in his spiritual growth—and Timothy responded. In fact, Timothy responded so well that Paul took him on the rest of his missionary journey, and Timothy helped produce spiritual fruit within a number of churches.

But things don't always proceed at that pace. Not even when Paul is your disciple-maker:

> 1 For my part, brothers and sisters, I was not able to speak to you as
> spiritual people but as people of the flesh, as babies in Christ. 2 I gave you
> milk to drink, not solid food, since you were not yet ready for it. In fact,
> you are still not ready, 3 because you are still worldly. For since there is
> envy and strife among you, are you not worldly and behaving like mere
> humans?
> 1 CORINTHIANS 3:1-3

The Christians in the city of Corinth were much slower in their development than Timothy. They lived in a city filled with all kinds of promiscuity, and they did not have the benefit of godly parents and grandparents, as Timothy did. Consequently, their spiritual growth was a much more gradual process. But Paul continued to invest. He continued to guide them as a spiritual father toward maturity.

May we do the same with those in our spiritual care.

PERSONAL STUDY

SPIRITUAL GUIDANCE

We've seen already in this session that different disciples will live at different stages of spiritual growth along their journey of following Christ. We've also seen that different people will progress through those stages at different speeds. These are important truths, because they help us know how to provide spiritual guidance to those we serve as disciple-makers.

Look, for example, at what the author of Hebrews wrote to some of the disciples under his care:

> [11] We have a great deal to say about this, and it is difficult to explain, since
> you have become too lazy to understand. [12] Although by this time you
> ought to be teachers, you need someone to teach you the basic principles
> of God's revelation again. You need milk, not solid food. [13] Now everyone
> who lives on milk is inexperienced with the message about righteousness,
> because he is an infant. [14] But solid food is for the mature—for those
> whose senses have been trained to distinguish between good and evil.
>
> [1] Therefore, let us leave the elementary teaching about Christ and go on
> to maturity, not laying again a foundation of repentance from dead works,
> faith in God, [2] teaching about ritual washings, laying on of hands, the
> resurrection of the dead, and eternal judgment. [3] And we will do this if
> God permits.
> HEBREWS 5:11–6:3

What strikes you as most interesting from these verses? Why?

Who in your life has given you this kind of personal spiritual direction?

Notice that the author of Hebrews wanted to see these disciples move to a new stage of spiritual development. He wanted them to keep progressing in their journey toward spiritual maturity—and he wanted *them* to desire that growth, as well. Yet he was also aware of their spiritual sluggishness. He knew they were not progressing quickly, and he sought to guide them into a greater sense of urgency about their own spiritual lives.

Notice also that this disciple-maker had a good awareness of what these disciples knew, and what they didn't know. The Book of Hebrews was written to Jewish Christians, many of whom were struggling with letting go of the law and their old patterns of religion. The author of Hebrews knew they had a good foundation in terms of what they'd been taught about key doctrines—repentance, Jesus' resurrection, eternal judgment, and so on.

The author of Hebrews didn't want to cover old ground at this point. He wanted to guide the disciples in his care to a deeper engagement with the truths of God's Word.

What are some ways to assess your own stage of spiritual development?

What are some appropriate ways to evaluate the spiritual development of others?

Now, although the author of Hebrews did not want to re-cover old ground with these particular disciples, it's important to remember that repetition is a helpful (and often overlooked) method of discipleship. We are flawed human beings, which means we easily forget what we've heard. We need to be reminded about critical truths several times before they stick.

Jesus knew this to be true, which is why He often repeated important truths to His own disciples.

Read the following passages of Scripture. What does Jesus teach in each one?

Mark 8:31

Mark 9:31

Mark 10:33-34

What are the primary truths or doctrines that most disciples need to hear again and again?

SESSION 11

STRONG RELATIONSHIPS

Disciple-making requires serious, purposeful relationships for your own growth and the growth of others.

GET STARTED

REFLECT

In the previous session, we saw an effective model of disciple-making through the examples of Paul and Timothy. In order to be effective disciple-makers, we must be willing to make a substantial commitment to those in our spiritual care.

This session picks up where the last session left off. We'll explore an Old Testament model for disciple-making, and in doing so we'll see the value of strong relationships within that process. Before we move forward, however, take a few moments to talk about what you've experienced in the past week.

Which of the assignments did you explore this week? How did it go?

What did you learn or experience while reading the Bible?

What questions would you like to ask?

PRAY

Begin this session by connecting with God through prayer. Use the following guidelines as you speak with Him together:

- Express your gratitude to God for allowing you to serve as a disciple-maker.
- Proclaim that Jesus is the model for all disciple-makers, and ask Him to continue to reveal Himself to you as you strive to follow His example.
- Ask God for wisdom as you engage the Bible and learn why strong relationships are a key element in making disciples.

INTRODUCTION

In 1984, a film called *The Karate Kid* came out of nowhere to dominate the Hollywood box office. It earned more money that year than several other high-profile movies, including *Star Trek III: The Search for Spock*, *Purple Rain*, and the classic baseball flick, *The Natural*.

The Karate Kid tells the story of a young teenage boy who's being bullied by a group of peers in his new hometown. A pivotal scene occurs early in the movie when Daniel, the main character, gets beaten up by a group of boys from a local karate dojo. Just as Daniel is at the point of passing out, an elderly gardener, Mr. Miyagi, leaps into the fray and scatters the young attackers. Daniel is astonished by what he sees, and he asks the old gardener to teach him how to fight.

Mr. Miyagi promises to teach Daniel karate as a means of self-defense. And that's when the movie transforms from a story about boys and conflict to a study on the relationship between a mentor and his mentee.

The relationship between Daniel and Mr. Miyagi is more than a friendship; it's more than a coach training a player or a guide taking someone on a great adventure. Their relationship is strategic, personal, and purposeful. In many ways, it's a relationship that mirrors much of what can happen (and should happen) between disciple-makers and disciples.

What are some of your favorite mentor/mentee relationships from fiction or from history?

When have you been part of such a relationship?

As we'll see in this session, discipleship relationships work best when everyone involved understands their roles in the disciple-making process. Without such an understanding, our attempts at discipleship often deteriorate into just another friendship with no eternal significance.

KNOW THE STORY

Discipleship relationships are like no other connection you've experienced. They're transformational, rather than informational. They require people to do life together in a way that cannot stay on the surface. They go deep. We can find an example of such a relationship in the Old Testament when we explore the connection between Elijah and Elisha.

15 Then the LORD said to him, "Go and return by the way you
came to the Wilderness of Damascus. When you arrive, you are
to anoint Hazael as king over Aram. 16 You are to anoint Jehu
son of Nimshi as king over Israel and Elisha son of Shaphat from
Abel-meholah as prophet in your place. 17 Then Jehu will put to
death whoever escapes the sword of Hazael, and Elisha will put
to death whoever escapes the sword of Jehu. 18 But I will leave
seven thousand in Israel—every knee that has not bowed to
Baal and every mouth that has not kissed him."

19 Elijah left there and found Elisha son of Shaphat as he was
plowing. Twelve teams of oxen were in front of him, and he
was with the twelfth team. Elijah walked by him and threw his
mantle over him. 20 Elisha left the oxen, ran to follow Elijah, and
said, "Please let me kiss my father and mother, and then I will
follow you."

"Go on back," he replied, "for what have I done to you?"

21 So he turned back from following him, took the team of oxen,
and slaughtered them. With the oxen's wooden yoke and plow,
he cooked the meat and gave it to the people, and they ate. Then
he left, followed Elijah, and served him.
1 KINGS 19:15-21

What do you find most surprising in these verses? Why?

What can we learn about Elijah and Elisha from this passage?

UNPACK THE STORY

DISCIPLESHIP IS SERIOUS

Our world today is filled with casual relationships. We all have acquaintances and casual connections in our work and in our communities—people we know and like, but who don't factor deeply in our lives. Even at church, and even in a group setting, few of our connections go below the surface.

Given this reality in our culture, it's important to understand there's nothing casual about discipleship. When we enter into a disciple-making relationship, we must do so with a seriousness of purpose. We must be willing to make a serious commitment. And that's one of the things we see in the example of Elijah and Elisha.

Look back at 1 Kings 19:15-21. Where do you see evidence of a seriousness commitment between Elijah and Elisha?

What are some serious commitments you've currently made to other people?

It's important to understand there's nothing casual about discipleship.

The first thing to understand about Elijah's efforts to mentor Elisha is that it wasn't his idea. God specifically directed Elijah to approach the younger man and take him under his wing for the specific purpose of training Elisha as God's next prophet.

Our efforts at disciple-making should follow the same principle. That doesn't mean we should wait until we hear God's voice audibly commanding us to connect with someone. But it does mean that our discipleship efforts should be in submission to the Holy Spirit and bathed in prayer. When we feel drawn to another person and sense their potential, we should seek God's will and the Spirit's approval before we move forward.

The second thing to understand about Elijah and Elisha was the official nature of their relationship. Right from the start, Elijah walked to the younger man and "threw his mantle over him." This "mantle" was a piece of clothing—a robe or other item that specifically pointed to Elijah's role as a prophet. By transferring that mantle to Elisha, the older man was officially signaling his desire to transfer the role of prophet, as well.

It's worth repeating: there's nothing casual about discipleship. The relationship between disciple-maker and disciple works best when each person understands his or her role.

DISCIPLESHIP REQUIRES SACRIFICE

Engaging a lifestyle of discipleship means making serious commitments and taking up an official role within the body of Christ. That means we need to count the cost.

How will a commitment to discipleship impact your life?

In addition, engaging a lifestyle of discipleship means making serious sacrifices. We see that in the interaction between Elijah and Elisha. Specifically, the text makes a point to mention Elisha's "twelve teams of oxen" (v. 19). That detail in particular would have caught the attention of anyone in the ancient world. Twelve teams of oxen was a lot of oxen, which meant Elisha must have been plowing a huge amount of farmland, which meant he was expecting a huge harvest at the end of his efforts.

Basically, the Scripture is telling us that Elisha was part of a wealthy family. He had a very comfortable situation, and he had every expectation of looking forward to a safe and prosperous future.

Elijah understood he was calling the younger man to give up that future, and it stung him: "'Go on back,' he replied, 'for what have I done to you?'" (v. 20). But Elisha left no room for uncertainty about his desire to be discipled:

> So he turned back from following him, took the team of oxen, and slaughtered them. With the oxen's wooden yoke and plow, he cooked the meat and gave it to the people, and they ate. Then he left, followed Elijah, and served him.
> 1 KINGS 19:21

Engaging a lifestyle of discipleship means making serious sacrifices.

What are some sacrifices you will need to make in order to be discipled?

What are some sacrifices you will need to make in order to be a disciple-maker?

ENGAGE

We've seen that a lifestyle of discipleship will require serious commitment and a willingness to sacrifice. One resource that connects with both of those factors is time. Use the circle below to make a pie chart showing how much time you spend on the major pieces of your life in a given week—work, sleep, family time, entertainment, commuting, and so on.

Where can you make sacrifices in order to carve out more time for your commitment to discipleship?

PRAYER REQUESTS

WEEKLY ACTIVITIES

In addition to studying God's Word, work with your group leader to create a plan for personal study, worship, and application between now and the next session. Select from the following optional activities to match your personal preferences and available time.

Worship

- [x] Read your Bible. Complete the reading plan on page 154.

- [ ] Spend time with God by engaging the devotional experience on page 155.

Personal Study

- [ ] Read and interact with "Three Key Practices" on page 156.

- [ ] Read and interact with "The Disciple-Makers Goal" on page 158.

Application

- [ ] Memorize Luke 9:62: "But Jesus said to him, 'No one who puts his hand to the plow and looks back is fit for the kingdom of God.'"

- [ ] Continue making and praying through a list of people that God may be calling you to disciple—or whom you have been drawn to as a potential disciple-maker in your life. Seek God's will for your involvement in the discipleship process.

- [ ] Begin reaching out to some of the individuals on your list. Start by asking them to get together for coffee or a meal. Seek to deepen those relationships and look for confirmation that God desires you to move forward toward an official discipleship connection.

- [ ] Take whatever steps are necessary to free up some time in your schedule each week. It may be especially helpful to intentionally block out time on your calendar to be used for discipling others or being discipled yourself.

- [ ] Other:

WORSHIP

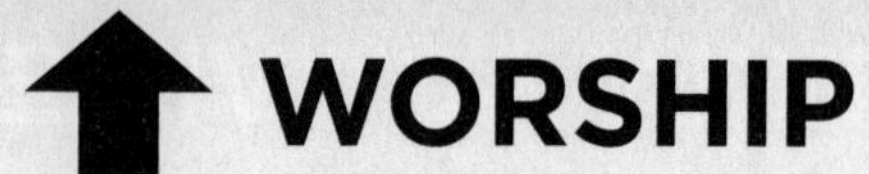

READING PLAN

Read through the following Scripture passages this week. Use the space provided to record your thoughts and responses.

Day 1
1 Timothy 1:12-20

Day 2
1 Timothy 4:6-16

Day 3
1 Timothy 6:1-10

Day 4
1 Timothy 6:11-21

Day 5
2 Timothy 1:1-12

Day 6
2 Timothy 2:1-26

Day 7
2 Timothy 4:1-18

COUNT THE COST

Jesus taught about the sacrifice that's required for us to follow Him as disciples—and to lead others in doing the same. In fact, Jesus' teachings were shocking to those who heard Him:

> 25 Now great crowds were traveling with him. So he turned and said to them:
> 26 "If anyone comes to me and does not hate his own father and mother, wife
> and children, brothers and sisters—yes, and even his own life—he cannot be
> my disciple. 27 Whoever does not bear his own cross and come after me cannot
> be my disciple.
>
> 28 "For which of you, wanting to build a tower, doesn't first sit down and
> calculate the cost to see if he has enough to complete it? 29 Otherwise, after
> he has laid the foundation and cannot finish it, all the onlookers will begin to
> ridicule him, 30 saying, 'This man started to build and wasn't able to finish.'
>
> 31 "Or what king, going to war against another king, will not first sit down and
> decide if he is able with ten thousand to oppose the one who comes against
> him with twenty thousand? 32 If not, while the other is still far off, he sends a
> delegation and asks for terms of peace. 33 In the same way, therefore, every one
> of you who does not renounce all his possessions cannot be my disciple."
> LUKE 14:25-33

How should we understand Jesus' use of the word "hate" in these verses?

What are some ways relationships can pull us away from living as Jesus' disciples and striving to make more disciples?

What are some ways possessions can pull us away from living as Jesus' disciples and striving to make more disciples?

PERSONAL STUDY

THREE KEY PRACTICES

When Paul described his ministry as a church-planter and disciple-maker in the city of Colossae, he wrote these words:

> We proclaim him, warning and teaching everyone with all wisdom, so that we may present everyone mature in Christ. I labor for this, striving with his strength that works powerfully in me.
> COLOSSIANS 1:28-29

That word "mature" points to our goal as disciple-makers. It refers to someone who is full grown, adult, or of full age. The goal of a spiritual parent is to present those they disciple to Christ as fully mature followers who have grown from spiritual infants into spiritual adults, capable of reproducing more disciples on their own.

What are some other characteristics that identify someone as a mature, fully grown disciple of Jesus?

In 1 Thessalonians, when Paul described his relationship with the people who made up the church in Thessalonica, he gave us another window into his methods for discipleship:

> [10] You are witnesses, and so is God, of how devoutly, righteously, and
> blamelessly we conducted ourselves with you believers. [11] As you know,
> like a father with his own children, [12] we encouraged, comforted, and
> implored each one of you to live worthy of God, who calls you into his own
> kingdom and glory.
> 1 THESSALONIANS 2:10-12

What do you like best about these verses? Why?

What can we learn from these verses about the process of discipleship?

As Paul pointed out, a spiritual parent takes three specific actions when helping his or her spiritual children mature in Christ: encourage, comfort, and implore.

First, we encourage. In this context, to encourage is to appeal to the spiritual child you're discipling. This practice includes guiding the disciple to obey God's expectations, but it also means intentionally offering reassurance throughout the process. The encouragement you give will allow the disciple to gain confidence as he or she presses ahead in the process.

Second, it's important for disciple-makers to comfort the spiritual children they're discipling. In this connotation, to comfort is to reassure a disciple so that he or she will stay the course. Comforting denotes the affectionate and compassionate counsel of a loving, caring father. When giving comfort, it's important to exhibit a compassionate love rather than exercising a stern authority.

Third, we implore. This happens when we passionately and emphatically urge disciples to move forward or take a necessary step. As spiritual parents, we often know what's necessary for spiritual growth. We have experience on our side. Therefore, there are times when it's appropriate for us to earnestly make an appeal to a disciple and direct them toward a right decision.

How confident do you feel in your ability to encourage others?

How confident do you feel in your ability to comfort others?

How confident do you feel in your ability to implore others?

As a disciple-maker, always remember that your role is primary relational. You're not just a "leader" for the person or people you're discipling. You're a friend. You're a spiritual parent.

In this way, you have a tremendous opportunity to make a positive impact not only in the life of a disciple, but for the kingdom of God. Discipleship is what Jesus had in mind for His church all along. It's the backbone of our growth and development as followers of Christ.

THE DISCIPLE-MAKER'S GOAL

We saw earlier in this session that Elijah and Elisha offer an interesting example of mentoring and discipleship in the Old Testament. As we continue forward with their story, we'll find an important reminder of what our goal should be when we serve as disciple-makers in the name of Jesus.

By the time we jump to 2 Kings 2, Elijah is nearing the end of his life. In fact, he knows he is living out his very last day on earth. That leads to some interesting interactions with his disciple, Elisha.

Read 2 Kings 2:1-6. What are some possible reasons why Elijah wanted his young disciple to go elsewhere at this moment?

What are some possible reasons why Elisha refused to leave?

Finally, we reach the moment of truth:

> 7 Fifty men from the sons of the prophets came and stood observing them
> at a distance while the two of them stood by the Jordan. 8 Elijah took his
> mantle, rolled it up, and struck the water, which parted to the right and
> left. Then the two of them crossed over on dry ground. 9 When they had
> crossed over, Elijah said to Elisha, "Tell me what I can do for you before I
> am taken from you."
>
> So Elisha answered, "Please, let me inherit two shares of your spirit."
>
> 10 Elijah replied, "You have asked for something difficult. If you see me
> being taken from you, you will have it. If not, you won't."
>
> 11 As they continued walking and talking, a chariot of fire with horses of
> fire suddenly appeared and separated the two of them. Then Elijah went
> up into heaven in the whirlwind. 12a As Elisha watched, he kept crying out,
> "My father, my father, the chariots and horsemen of Israel!"
>
> 2 KINGS 2:7-12a

Elisha's request to "inherit two shares" of Elijah's spirit is important. In the ancient world, a father's first-born son received a double portion for his inheritance to show that he would carry his father's authority and lead the family after the father was gone. Therefore, Elisha was essentially asking Elijah to recognize him not only as God's next prophet, but as Elijah's spiritual son.

Then, all of a sudden, Elijah was gone. This is a critical moment in the life of any disciple. What will he or she do once it's time to "move out of the house" in a spiritual sense? Will the disciple falter and fall away when he or she is no longer directly under the care of a disciple-maker? Or will the disciple stand strong and continue forward in the process of discipleship?

We can see how that question was answered in Elisha's case:

> 12b When he could see him no longer, he took hold of his own clothes, tore
> them in two, 13 picked up the mantle that had fallen off Elijah, and went
> back and stood on the bank of the Jordan. 14 He took the mantle Elijah
> had dropped, and he struck the water. "Where is the LORD God of Elijah?"
> he asked. He struck the water himself, and it parted to the right and the
> left, and Elisha crossed over.
>
> 2 KINGS 2:12b-14

What actions does Elisha take to prove his willingness to follow in Elijah's footsteps?

How does God confirm Elisha's spiritual maturity and readiness for the tasks ahead?

As disciple-makers, we need to have a goal in mind as we do the work of disciple-making. And that goal is simply that those in our spiritual care would develop into mature, fully capable disciples of Jesus Christ. It's not likely that we'll be caught up to heaven in a chariot of fire, as was the case with Elijah. But it's absolutely certain that we won't be around forever—and that we won't be able to maintain the same level of guidance and support with our disciples indefinitely.

In the end, we will need to let go and allow new disciples of Jesus to carry on the work of discipleship.

SESSION 12

WHO IS A DISCIPLE-MAKER?

Every Christian can have a lifestyle of discipleship. And every Christian should

GET STARTED

REFLECT

As we saw in the previous session, discipleship is relational. Both disciple-makers and disciples have specific roles to carry out in the process of growing toward spiritual maturity, and it's critical for all people involved to be both committed and purposeful in those relationships.

As you prepare to dive into the final teaching session of this resource, take some time to share what you've experienced since the last gathering.

Which of the assignments did you explore this week? How did it go?

What did you learn or experience while reading the Bible?

What questions would you like to ask?

PRAY

Begin this session by connecting with God through prayer. Use the following guidelines as you speak with Him together:

- Thank God for the opportunities you've been given to engage the process of discipleship, both as a disciple and a disciple-maker.
- Acknowledge your understanding that God has put you in your current situation and circumstances for a purpose.
- Pray for wisdom and guidance as you seek to engage new opportunities for discipleship in the months and years ahead.

INTRODUCTION

Each year, several thousand people take their first step on a 2,176 mile journey. For the most part, these are people just like you—the same kinds of people you see at the movie theater, at church, at sporting events, and so on. But these people in particular have made the choice to hike the Appalachian Trail.

If you're one of the lucky ones, the Appalachian Trail is a five-month march. It begins at Springer Mountain, Georgia, and ends at Mt. Katahdin in Maine. Paul Stutzman, in his book *Hiking Through,* described the journey like this:

> If you are ever one of those solitary Appalachian Trail thru-hikers and you somehow survive three hundred daunting mountains, precarious river crossings, difficult rock climbs, discouraging illness and loneliness, and punishing weather, and you stand at last at the summit of mighty Mt. Katahdin, then you will indeed know what it is to be one of those chosen few. You are then forever part of the brotherhood and sisterhood of the Appalachian Trail.[1]

Of the thousands who attempt this hike each year, only hundreds succeed in finishing it. Those who do have a few things in common.

First, they have a vision. They can clearly see themselves standing at the end of the Appalachian Trail, having completed the seemingly impossible task set before them. Second, they believe in their heart of hearts that they're capable of accomplishing something that extraordinary. Instead of talking themselves out of a great adventure by telling themselves, "Not me," they ask themselves, "Why not me?" Third, they courageously take the first step.

What's an adventure you've always wanted to try?

What are some spiritual goals that seem out of reach right now?

In this session, we'll see what can happen when everyday disciples have a vision of being useful in God's kingdom, believe they can do the work of discipleship, and take their first step on that amazing journey.

KNOW THE STORY

Regular church members often believe they're not capable of doing significant work for God's kingdom. As we'll see in the Book of Acts, however, nothing could be further from the truth.

18 After staying for some time, Paul said farewell to the brothers
and sisters and sailed away to Syria, accompanied by Priscilla
and Aquila. He shaved his head at Cenchreae because of a
vow he had taken. 19 When they reached Ephesus he left them
there, but he himself entered the synagogue and debated with
the Jews. 20 When they asked him to stay for a longer time, he
declined, 21 but he said farewell and added, "I'll come back to
you again, if God wills." Then he set sail from Ephesus.

22 On landing at Caesarea, he went up to Jerusalem and greeted
the church, then went down to Antioch. 23 After spending some
time there, he set out, traveling through one place after another in
the region of Galatia and Phrygia, strengthening all the disciples.

24 Now a Jew named Apollos, a native Alexandrian, an eloquent
man who was competent in the use of the Scriptures, arrived in
Ephesus. 25 He had been instructed in the way of the Lord; and
being fervent in spirit, he was speaking and teaching accurately
about Jesus, although he knew only John's baptism. 26 He began
to speak boldly in the synagogue. After Priscilla and Aquila
heard him, they took him aside and explained the way of God to
him more accurately. 27 When he wanted to cross over to Achaia,
the brothers and sisters wrote to the disciples to welcome him.
After he arrived, he was a great help to those who by grace
had believed. 28 For he vigorously refuted the Jews in public,
demonstrating through the Scriptures that Jesus is the Messiah.
ACTS 18:18-28

What's your first impression of each person mentioned in these verses?

How do these verses highlight the power of discipleship?

UNPACK THE STORY

GOD USES EVERYDAY PEOPLE TO MAKE DISCIPLES

Priscilla and Aquila were tent-makers by trade. Unlike Paul and Apollos, they weren't public figures who made a splash in the streets and synagogues. They weren't professional preachers, they didn't write books, and they didn't have a marketing platform to speak of.

Yet they made a difference. For one thing, the apostle Paul stayed with them in their home for a year and a half. They also invited Apollos to stay with them as he began to burst onto the public scene. So, Priscilla and Aquila were Jesus-centered believers who exhibited Christ-like love through the ministry of hospitality.

Who is a Priscilla or Aquila in your church—someone who serves faithfully in the background and makes a difference?

How has your spiritual journey been influenced by the help and support of lay leaders?

Priscilla and Aquila were Jesus-centered believers who exhibited Christ-like love through the ministry of hospitality.

That wasn't all they accomplished, however. Priscilla and Aquila also took on some weighty responsibilities. They traveled with Paul on his missionary journey, for example. And when Paul moved on from Ephesus, he left them there to continue his evangelistic work in that city. They were lay people, but they were key leaders in the Ephesian church.

Evidently, Priscilla and Aquila didn't stay in Ephesus, because Paul sent greetings to them when he wrote to the church in Rome. And look at what he wrote:

> 3 Give my greetings to Prisca and Aquila, my coworkers in Christ
> Jesus, 4 who risked their own necks for my life. Not only do I
> thank them, but so do all the Gentile churches. 5 Greet also the
> church that meets in their home.
> ROMANS 16:3-5a

Like most people, you probably see yourself as a "Regular Joe" or a "Regular Jane." You're likely aware of your shortcomings, for the most part, and you understand that you're not perfect. All of this is excellent when it comes to discipleship. Why? Because knowing your limitations will help you to take a backseat in your life and allow the Holy Spirit to empower to accomplish great things for God's kingdom.

ALL DISCIPLE-MAKERS ARE EQUAL

Shifting the focus to Apollos, it's clear that he was a gifted speaker and church leader. The text describes him as "an eloquent man who was competent in the use of the Scriptures" (Acts 18:24). Interestingly, that word translated "competent" can also mean "powerful." Apollos was bold and influential; he was the furthest thing from average.

In fact, Apollos made such an impression in the early church that many Christians in the city of Corinth elevated him to a status above Paul. (See 1 Corinthians 1:11-12.) This was a mistake on the Corinthians' part, of course, since all Christians are followers of Christ alone. Yet it shows the influence Apollos had in the church.

Given that reality, look again at Apollos' interaction with Priscilla and Aquila:

> [25] [Apollos] had been instructed in the way of the Lord; and
> being fervent in spirit, he was speaking and teaching accurately
> about Jesus, although he knew only John's baptism. [26] He began
> to speak boldly in the synagogue. After Priscilla and Aquila
> heard him, they took him aside and explained the way of God to
> him more accurately.
> ACTS 18:25-26

True disciple-makers live in submission to Christ, and Christ alone.

What does this incident reveal about Priscilla and Aquila? About Apollos?

Who is currently making a difference for God's kingdom in your church and/or community?

How can you contribute to that good work?

Apollos, Priscilla, and Aquila all understood that disciple-makers are on equal footing. That's because true disciple-makers live in submission to Christ, and Christ alone. We are all servants of our Master, which means we are all on the same team, working toward the same goals, and empowered by the same Holy Spirit.

ENGAGE

We've seen that regular, everyday people can make a tremendous difference in God's kingdom. But it's necessary for us to be fueled by the Holy Spirit before anything positive will take place. With that in mind, spend several minutes in prayer, asking the Holy Spirit to empower you and the other members of your group to accomplish His work according to His will.

When helpful, use the following questions to prompt your prayers.

How will you submit yourself to God's will, rather than your will?

What fears do you need to let go?

What are your hopes for your own spiritual growth? For your congregation and community?

PRAYER REQUESTS

1. Paul Stutzman, *Hiking Through* (Grand Rapids: Revell, 2012), p. 33.

WEEKLY ACTIVITIES

In addition to studying God's Word, work with your group leader to create a plan for personal study, worship, and application between now and the next session. Select from the following optional activities to match your personal preferences and available time.

Worship

- [x] Read your Bible. Complete the reading plan on page 168.
- [ ] Spend time with God by engaging the devotional experience on page 169.

Personal Study

- [ ] Read and interact with "No Ordinary Spirit" on page 170.
- [ ] Read and interact with "No Ordinary Body" on page 172.

Application

- [ ] Memorize Philippians 4:19: "And my God will supply all your needs according to his riches in glory in Christ Jesus."
- [ ] Look back on your journey over the last 12 sessions by skimming through your Personal Study Guide. Write down those things you want to be certain you remember as you continue your journey as a disciple-maker.
- [ ] Continue to pray daily for those God has brought into your spheres of influence, whether as a potential disciple or disciple-maker.
- [ ] Continue to get in touch with those people to see where God leads in terms of present and/or future disciple-making relationships.
- [ ] Other:

WORSHIP

READING PLAN

Read through the following Scripture passages this week. Use the space provided to record your thoughts and responses.

Day 1
Matthew 26:6-13

Day 2
Acts 6:8–7:60

Day 3
Genesis 26:1-35

Day 4
Acts 9:1-19

Day 5
1 Samuel 17:1-50

Day 6
Exodus 1:8-21

Day 7
Luke 24:1-12

JOINING THE TEAM

As we approach the end of this journey called *Disciples Path,* it's essential that we remember where we started. All our efforts at discipleship start with one statement—one expectation of Jesus that is often called "The Great Commission."

Here it is in full:

> [18] Jesus came near and said to them, "All authority has been given to me
> in heaven and on earth. [19] Go, therefore, and make disciples of all nations,
> baptizing them in the name of the Father and of the Son and of the Holy Spirit,
> [20] teaching them to observe everything I have commanded you. And remember,
> I am with you always, to the end of the age."
> MATTHEW 28:18-20

You'll notice that this statement is called a "commission." Unlike many of Jesus' declared expectations, which are often called commandments, the church calls this pronouncement a "commission." That's important.

To be commissioned is to be authorized by someone in authority to do something. Jesus was telling His disciples, and every believer that would become one of His followers throughout human history, that He has authorized them to make more disciples. That is our mission as members of God's kingdom. That is our Great Commission.

***How has your understanding of this Great Commission changed throughout your journey with* Disciples Path?**

What will you do in the coming week to obey this commission?

What will you do in the coming year to obey this commission?

NO ORDINARY SPIRIT

When we think of ordinary people living as disciples of Jesus, we don't have to look any further than Jesus' original disciples. Those twelve men had "regular guys" written all over them. Several of them were fishermen, for example—blue-collar workers following in the family business. We know Matthew was originally a tax collector who, before his encounter with Jesus, had a penchant for greed. Most scholars believe the rest of Jesus' disciples were simple tradesmen.

That begs an important question: what turned those ordinary men into revolutionaries who transformed the world forever? The answer is they were empowered by the Holy Spirit. They accomplished incredible things because they were ordinary people carried along by an extraordinary God.

The good news, of course, is that Christians today have access to that same Spirit. We've covered this topic on several occasions throughout *Disciples Path: The Journey,* but it's worth taking another look at how the Spirit fuels every aspect of our lives.

Read through the following passages of Scripture and record what they teach about the Spirit's role in our everyday lives:

Ezekiel 36:26-27

John 14:25-26

Acts 1:7-8

Romans 8:26-27

Galatians 5:22-26

Every follower of Jesus has been blessed by the indwelling of the Holy Spirit—including yourself. You carry God's Spirit inside of you, which makes you His temple (see 1 Corinthians 3:16-17). There's nothing ordinary about that!

One of the most wonderful aspects of the Holy Spirit's work in our lives is they way He removes our doubts and fears when we rely on His power. That's important when it comes to the practice of disciple-making. Why? Because the practice of disciple-making makes a lot of Christians feel afraid.

What fears come to mind when you consider serving as a disciple-maker within your church and community? List three.

1.

2.

3.

Philip's encounter with the Ethiopian official offers an encouraging glimpse into how the Spirit can guide our steps.

Read Acts 8:26-40. Where do you see evidence of the Holy Spirit's guidance as Philip sought to make a new disciple?

How have you experienced the guidance of the Holy Spirit in your regular routines and schedules?

How would you like to experience the Spirit's guidance in your efforts to make disciples?

If you are a disciple of Jesus, you are no ordinary disciple-maker. You have access to the incredible power of the Holy Spirit. He is always willing to do His work of making disciples through us if we will simply trust Him and allow Him to speak through us.

PERSONAL STUDY 2

NO ORDINARY BODY

Another obstacle that often prevents disciples of Jesus from becoming mature disciple-makers is a perceived lack of wisdom. We worry that we're not wise enough, smart enough, influential enough, or significant enough to help others move toward spiritual maturity.

However, according to God's Word, our lack of wisdom is *exactly* what qualifies us to go out and make disciples in the name of Christ:

> 26 Brothers and sisters, consider your calling: Not many were wise from
> a human perspective, not many powerful, not many of noble birth.
> 27 Instead, God has chosen what is foolish in the world to shame the
> wise, and God has chosen what is weak in the world to shame the
> strong. 28 God has chosen what is insignificant and despised in the world
> —what is viewed as nothing—to bring to nothing what is viewed as
> something, 29 so that no one may boast in his presence. 30 It is from him
> that you are in Christ Jesus, who became wisdom from God for us—our
> righteousness, sanctification, and redemption, 31 in order that, as it is
> written: Let the one who boasts, boast in the Lord.
> 1 CORINTHIANS 1:26-31

What's your initial reaction to this passage? Why?

Which of the weaknesses listed in these verses resonate with you?

What steps can you take to "boast in the Lord" as you do the work of making disciples?

Another reason many people struggle to see themselves as disciple-makers is because they compare themselves with other believers. When we do this, the enemy whispers discouragement to our hearts: "You're not worthy." "You're not as capable as other people are." "You're much lower on the church totem pole than everyone else."

Thankfully, God has spoken truth through His Word to remind us that all Christians are equal because we're all part of the same body.

> 12 For just as the body is one and has many parts, and all the parts of that
> body, though many, are one body—so also is Christ. 13 For we were all
> baptized by one Spirit into one body—whether Jews or Greeks, whether
> slaves or free—and we were all given one Spirit to drink. 14 Indeed, the
> body is not one part but many. 15 If the foot should say, "Because I'm not
> a hand, I don't belong to the body," it is not for that reason any less a part
> of the body. 16 And if the ear should say, "Because I'm not an eye, I don't
> belong to the body," it is not for that reason any less a part of the body.
> 17 If the whole body were an eye, where would the hearing be? If the whole
> body were an ear, where would the sense of smell be? 18 But as it is, God
> has arranged each one of the parts in the body just as he wanted. 19 And if
> they were all the same part, where would the body be? 20 As it is, there are
> many parts, but one body. 21 The eye cannot say to the hand, "I don't need
> you!" Or again, the head can't say to the feet, "I don't need you!" 22 On the
> contrary, those parts of the body that are weaker are indispensable. 23 And
> those parts of the body that we consider less honorable, we clothe these
> with greater honor, and our unrespectable parts are treated with greater
> respect, 24 which our respectable parts do not need.
>
> Instead, God has put the body together, giving greater honor to the less
> honorable, 25 so that there would be no division in the body, but that the
> members would have the same concern for each other. 26 So if one member
> suffers, all the members suffer with it; if one member is honored, all the
> members rejoice with it.
>
> 1 CORINTHIANS 12:12-26

Which of these verses catch your attention? Why?

What are we called to do when we believe these verses are true?

SESSION 13

REFLECT AND CONNECT

Conclude this journey on the "Disciples Path" with a time of review and fellowship as a group.

REFLECT

In the previous session, we addressed the question, "Who is a disciple-maker?" The answer is you. Everyone who follows Christ is called to follow Him in making disciples, which means you are a disciple-maker. And if you also happen to be a "regular" or "ordinary" person, than you are especially qualified to make disciples through the power of the Holy Spirit.

Which of the assignments did you explore this week? How did it go?

What did you learn or experience while reading the Bible?

What questions would you like to ask?

As you conclude Volume 4 of Disciples Path: The Journey, use this final session as an opportunity to review what you've learned and enjoy spending time together as a community. When helpful, use the following questions to guide your conversations.

What's an "Aha!" moment you experienced during the past 12 sessions?

How have you grown as a disciple of Jesus in the past year?

How have you grown as a disciple-maker?

Who is someone you would like to lead through Disciples Path: The Journey in order to help them develop as a disciple-maker?

PRAY

Finish your gathering by praying that God's Spirit would guide each of you to go out into your community and make disciples in the name of Jesus Christ.

YOUR JOURNEY IS JUST BEGINNING.

Spiritual maturity requires ongoing study of the Bible with a group of fellow believers. Now that you've completed *Disciples Path: The Journey*, here are some additional paths to consider.

DO YOU WANT TO STUDY THE BIBLE...

...BOOK BY BOOK?

Explore the Bible: Adults
LifeWay.com/ExploreTheBible

This book-by-book group Bible study takes participants deep into Scripture, revealing context essential to understanding the text's original intent, resulting in a framework for both knowing and living out God's Word in personal and transformative ways.

...THROUGH REAL-LIFE, EVERYDAY ISSUES?

Bible Studies for Life: Adults
BibleStudiesForLife.com

This resource connects God's Word to our lives in an intentional way. Over time, Bible Studies for Life helps adults grow in eight key, research-validated attributes of discipleship.

...AS ONE STORY THAT POINTS TO JESUS?

The Gospel Project for Adults
GospelProject.com

This chronological, Christ-centered Bible study examines how all Scripture gives testimony to Jesus Christ. Discover how God's plan of redemption unfolds throughout Scripture and still today, compelling us to join the mission of God.

LifeWay.com/GoAdults Learn more about your Bible study options.

DisciplesPath.com Or you can start a new Disciples Path group and become a disciple who makes disciples.